MW01258513

Praise for *Founders, Keepers*

"This master class in how to build a startup would have helped me avoid some of my biggest professional mistakes—I just wish it had come out years ago!"
—Jonathan Seelig, Cofounder, Akamai

"*Founders, Keepers* is the mirror every founder needs. It provides the frameworks we, as leaders, need to grow with our companies. It's nice to find a book that takes the theoretical and makes it generally applicable to real life."
—Matt Tait, Cofounder and CEO, Decimal

"Rich writes with the clarity of having coached some of the best founders. He brilliantly captures the internal struggles and strengths of founders and shows the path to success."
—Mårten Mickos, former CEO, MySQL and HackerOne

"*Founders, Keepers* shows just how hard it is to be a founder and do the most insane thing imaginable—create something out of nothing. Calling on 40 years of research and unique wisdom and full of practical and actionable solutions, this book should be required reading for founders who want to take their companies and themselves to the next level."
—Maynard Webb, Founder, Webb Investment Network; Director, Salesforce and Visa; and Bestselling Author

"*Founders, Keepers* helped me to understand my own leadership style, to have the humility to admit where I fell short and to learn and adapt as quickly as my startup grew. From a naive visionary to a manager of relationships and execution—nine years into my startup, I'm still here."
—Richard Mabey, Cofounder and CEO, Juro

"Rich has created *the* blueprint for founder growth and success. He shows founders how to survive their unique flaws, but more importantly how they can turn their creativity into massive impact. This is a book that every founder should read."
—Mitchell Amador, CEO, Immunefi

"This book is the definitive guide on what separates successful founders from the rest, and what the best founders do to beat the odds."
—Joe Davy, Founder and CEO, Banzai

"Rich has been the secret to success for hundreds of the best Silicon Valley founders. I grew up as a founder thanks to Rich. This book distills his wisdom from a lifetime dedicated to observing and nurturing the world's top founders over the last three decades. You're in for a treat."
—Sander Daniels, Founder, Groombuggy

"I wish I had this book 20 years ago. Every page was poignant and relevant."
—Joe Hyrkin, former CEO, Issuu, Inc., and Tech Investor/Advisor

Also by Tien Tzuo

Subscribed: Why the Subscription Model Will Be Your Company's Future—
and What to Do About It (with Gabe Weisert, 2018)

FOUNDERS
KEEPERS

Why Founders Are
Built to Fail, and What
It Takes to Succeed

Richard Hagberg, PhD, and Tien Tzuo
with Gabe Weisert

Matt Holt Books
An Imprint of BenBella Books, Inc.
Dallas, TX

Founders, Keepers copyright © 2025 by Rich Hagberg, Tien Tzuo, and Gabe Weisert

Matt Holt is an imprint of BenBella Books, Inc.
8080 N. Central Expressway
Suite 1700
Dallas, TX 75206
benbellabooks.com
Send feedback to feedback@benbellabooks.com

BenBella and *Matt Holt* are federally registered trademarks.

Printed in the United States of America
10 9 8 7 6 5 4 3 2 1

Library of Congress Control Number: 2024058440
ISBN 9781637746905 (hardcover)
ISBN 9781637746912 (electronic)

Editing by Lydia Choi
Copyediting by Scott Calamar
Proofreading by Lisa Story and Natalie Roth
Indexing by WordCo Indexing Services, Inc.
Text design and composition by PerfecType, Nashville, TN
Cover design by Morgan Carr
Printed by Lake Book Manufacturing

We dedicate this book to founders, and the people who put up with them.

CONTENTS

PART III: DEVELOPING THE SKILLS REQUIRED TO SCALE 125

FOREWORD

By Peter Fenton

F ounders are the gravitational center around which the entire entrepreneurial world rotates. There's a magic to founders—a spark that cannot be replicated or engineered. Their bravery to take that first step, moved by a relentless obsession with an idea and an audacious refusal to accept the status quo, enables them to create something entirely new from pure imagination.

The generative traits that make founders exceptional also make their journey uniquely challenging. The traditional leadership templates just don't apply. Founders, by their nature, are "spiky." They often excel disproportionately in vision, while other areas—execution or people management—may lag. And that's okay. As Peter Drucker said, "Wherever there are highs, there must be lows; wherever there are peaks, there must be valleys."

This tension—manifesting the unbridled power of a founder's vision with the realities of scaling—defines the role we play at Benchmark, our service to founders. Service means recognizing when founders need support, advocating for their vision, and, when necessary, helping them navigate the complexities of leadership. Too often the stresses of leading through scale oxidize the energy systems of a founder, compromising their—and by extension their company's—purpose, undermining the totality of what might be possible. More founders are lost to exhaustion and to loss of confidence

than to boldness and grandeur. Our commitment to the inexhaustible purpose that motivates the founder motivates everything we do.

I first met Rich Hagberg early in my career, during my time on the
board of Lithium. Lithium was at that critical inflection point where the
founder's ability to scale the business needed transformation. Another
board member, Richard Yanowitch, recommended Rich as someone who
could help. I'll admit: I was a skeptic of coaching in its traditional form
of outside-in platitudes. Too often the homogenized advice of the expert
"coach" only erodes the towering peaks of vision and ambition into worn-
down rolling hills of domesticated mediocrity. Rich shattered this view of
coaching for me. He met founders where they were—free of any mold or
cast. He engaged the raw data, the artifacts of their leadership, in rigorous and systematic ways. This allowed him to amplify their strengths and
navigate their challenges without stripping away their core. I was happy to
introduce him to Tien, a peculiar kind of inexhaustible visionary founder
in need of his own transformation.

Two aphorisms illuminate the success of the Rich/Tien partnership.
My partner Bob Kagle urged investing in "learn it alls" not "know it alls."
Tien embodied this, diving into his work with Rich arms outstretched,
eager to absorb everything. His openness allowed him to confront his own
demons with full vulnerability and understand their impact on the company. The second comes from Accel cofounder Arthur Patterson: "We're
only as good as our handlers." For coaching to succeed, there must be vulnerability and trust. If you doubt your coach is fully committed to your
success, the relationship is doomed. Tien gave Rich his complete trust, and
Rich honored it with his best work.

This book, *Founders, Keepers*, represents the culmination of decades
of insight and hard-won lessons. Rich's approach reflects the uniqueness
of founders and the importance of *embracing* rather than flattening their
spikes. It acknowledges the paradox of the founder: their strengths are
often their weaknesses, their vision is their greatest gift, and their growth
as leaders is a continuous process. It also provides something I believe to be

invaluable: a road map for founders to navigate the evolution from visionary to leader without losing the magic that makes them who they are.

To the founders reading this: Know that you are not alone in the unique
challenges you face. The very qualities that set you apart can also isolate
you. This book is a testament to the belief that your vision matters, and
with the right tools and support, you can lead your company to greatness
while staying true to yourself. You can learn how to defuse the time bomb.

For those who invest in and support founders: Let this book be a
reminder of the privilege we have to work with such exceptional people.
Our job is not to change them but to serve them, to nurture their vision,
and to help them thrive. There is no greater reward than seeing a founder
take their dream and turn it into a reality that impacts the world.

Rich and Tien have crafted something extraordinary here. *Founders,
Keepers* is not just a book; it's a celebration of what makes founders special
and a guide for how to protect and empower that uniqueness. To every
founder out there: God bless, Godspeed, and go change the world.

DEAR FOUNDER

I am a recovering founder. I fit the classic profile: high on vision, medium on relationships, and abysmal at execution. In other words, I'm part of the problem.

Fifteen years ago I started focusing my leadership coaching practice on founders, because I found that I could personally relate to my clients. I resemble the people I am seeking to help. A big part of my practice is telling them what I learned about being a founder but also how I screwed up and all the mistakes I made. After all, failure is just as instructive (if not more so) than success.

I'm also a psychologist with over 40 years of empirical research on founders, startups, and leadership. What brings all this data to life are the conversations I have with my clients—two founders trying to figure out the way forward together. That's why I wanted to write this book with Tien.

Tien and I got in touch in 2011 for the usual reason I get in touch with founders: things were starting to fall apart. Tien wasn't the only one who suspected that his leadership style might be contributing to the problem. So we generated a personality profile showing how his personality impacted his leadership, gathered a huge amount of comments and ratings from his employees and his investors (always a humbling process), and got to work on leveraging his strengths and addressing his weaknesses. Since then he has turned his company into a world-class enterprise (this is the guy who coined the phrase "Subscription Economy"), and he has become a popular teacher in his own right, mentoring dozens of young entrepreneurs over the years.

If you're a founder, you have an instinctive aversion to people in positions of authority telling you what to do. I know Tien and I both certainly do. We aim to do two things with this book: help you figure out your own leadership and personality tendencies, and then offer some concrete advice on how to improve as a leader based on your own strengths and weaknesses. That's it. It's not our job to talk down to you, or get overly academic, or offer up a bunch of reductive metaphors. It's our job to offer empirically based guidance, which you are of course free to take or leave.

This is the premise of this book: In order to grow your startup, you're going to have to grow as a person. The natural tendencies that might lead to your initial success won't get you to the promised land. You need to understand what constitutes an unsuccessful founder so that you can become a successful one. The book doesn't cover everything, but it should be enough to point you in some promising directions. If you've found it worthwhile and feel like you want to dive in more, then by all means, drop me a line.

—Rich

■ ■ ■

I am a recovering founder. I fit a slightly different profile: high on vision, low on relationships, and average at execution. In other words, I'm part of the problem.

Founders are ticking time bombs. We can be very clever and charismatic, but when it comes to installing the systems and processes you need to actually run a functional company, we don't always scale well. I certainly didn't. Three years after founding my company Zuora, there was plenty of growth, but burnout was high, morale was low, and turnover was turning into an issue. So at the request of my board member Peter Fenton, I submitted to a 360-degree review from a highly recommended organizational psychologist known as "Silicon Valley's CEO Whisperer." I found that of the eight characteristics of a great leader, I was in possession of a grand total of two.

And so began my 14-year journey with Rich.

What separates successful leaders from the rest? This is the question that Rich has been working on for almost his entire professional career. Over the last 15 years he has focused on founders. And he has the answers. They're not platitudes or sports metaphors or the stuff of self-help books. They're real. Rich has the data. In a way, this book is a summary of his life's work. It's also the result of hundreds of hours of conversation—most of them positive and constructive, some of them pretty tense, all of them brutally honest—between Rich and myself. I hope you find the conversation worthwhile. I know I do.

I could have been the typical narcissistic founder who gets fired as soon as my company gained real traction (you know the kind of people I'm talking about—you read about them every day). I was probably going down that path, but Rich's coaching process is basically like a mirror. It forces you to confront yourself: your strengths, your weaknesses, and what's holding you back. I credit my personal transformation, and Zuora's position today, to the insights that Rich has shared with me over the years.

I find Rich's research to be utterly unique and fascinating. It has inspired me to work with him to get it in the hands of as many people as possible. It's really important stuff. And it's all in this book.

—Tien

INTRODUCTION
The Ticking Time Bomb

The *Forbes* "30 Under 30" list has generated an impressive number of federal indictments.

Take Charlie Javice, who sold her student financial startup Frank to JPMorgan in 2021. She was indicted by the Justice Department for allegedly multiplying her customer count by an order of magnitude in order to facilitate the deal (she allegedly employed an outside data scientist to create a new "synthetic data set" of users).[1] Sam Bankman-Fried and his ex-CFO Caroline Ellison are also alumni of the *Forbes* list. So is Martin "Pharma Bro" Shkreli.[2] Elizabeth Holmes didn't make the cut, but *Forbes* gave her a special "Under 30 Doers Award" for her accomplishments at Theranos.[3] Trevor Milton, who made the *Forbes* "12 Under 40" list of young billionaires, founded a zero-emission truck company called Nikola Motor. He was convicted of fraud for (among other things) creating a demo video showing his nonfunctional vehicle rolling down a hill. The camera was tilted to make it look like a flat surface.[4]

A random sample of adults would result in far less evidence of blatant criminality. Most people are just not this felonious. What is going on here? Are these all uniquely bad people? Did they all have evil intentions from the start? (Putting aside Pharma Bro, that is.)

Probably not. Corporate crime is a step-by-step process. Law enforcement officials have a 10:10:80 rule of thumb when it comes to white-collar fraud: 10% of people would never commit fraud, 10% of people are actively seeking out opportunities to commit fraud, and 80% of people have the potential to commit fraud if the timing and circumstances are right. The vast majority of these founders probably started in the 80%, along with the rest of us.

As Bethany McLean, coauthor of the book *The Smartest Guys in the Room: The Amazing Rise and Scandalous Fall of Enron*, put it in an interview following the collapse of FTX: "It's very rare that you have one of the characters at the heart of this who actually understands . . . that they're moving over into the dark side and thinks about the potential repercussions of this and chooses this path anyway. That's usually not the way these stories go."[5]

So who's responsible? Let's not forget, all of these people were funded. They were all put in power by wealthy VC firms that pride themselves on their ability to identify dynamic, high-achieving founders capable of generating outsized returns. So are they to blame? Has the venture capital industry created an asshole industrial complex?

Again, probably not. Plenty of VC firms passed on Holmes and Bankman-Fried: their numbers were questioned, their research (or lack thereof) was found wanting. These firms pass on the vast majority of pitches they receive. They are well aware of the horrendous odds involved, the ungodly challenges, the crippling competition.

So what is going on here?

A Killing Field

The startup landscape is a killing field. Approximately 75% of venture-backed startups fail, meaning they fall short of reaching an exit at a valuation that would provide a return to all equity holders.[6] One study found that 50% of founders are still in control three years after their company launches, 40% after four years, and just a quarter of founders will remain if their company is one of the 2.5% who eventually IPO.[7]

How do startups die? Let us count the ways. You can have a great idea that's ahead of its time. An established incumbent can crush you with a copycat product. A competitor can offer 75% of what you do for 50% of the price (otherwise known as "disruption"). You can reach a certain altitude of revenue and then simply run out of oxygen. You can be undone by deceitful partners, feckless investors, indifferent employees. It's a cruel world out there.

Take the story of a founder who envisioned a social network exclusively for dog lovers: a space where they could share, connect, and perhaps even find love. But the dog lovers of the world, it turned out, were perfectly content with the social networks they were already using. The result? Three years of work with no pay down the drain. At least the founder still had their dog. It's a classic case of a solution wandering in search of a problem, a reminder that success in the startup world requires more than just a good idea—it demands that the market embrace that idea.

Financial hurdles are another nasty beast. The initial euphoria of funding quickly gives way to the harsh reality of burn rates. Picture a groundbreaking app, its launch on the horizon, only to be derailed by unforeseen coding costs or server fees. The project dies in the crib and winds up in bankruptcy. It's a stark lesson in the importance of meticulous financial planning and the brutal reality that in the world of startups, cash is both fuel and fire.

Then there's the battle against Goliaths—the established giants with their entrenched market shares and deep coffers. They can copy your innovations, gouge you on pricing, offer a "good enough" facsimile of your own service, and steal all your customers in the process.

Amid these external challenges lies the internal struggle—the dynamics of a team venturing into the unknown. Failure is always just around the corner. Your cofounder quits but keeps their equity. Your head of sales goes to a competitor. Your head of product decides to start a competing service. Infighting has killed sports teams, and startups are no different. A rift within the team can doom the entire venture.

Enter the Misfit

What kind of person willingly steps into this kind of hellscape? Who volunteers to play these kinds of odds? Successful or unsuccessful, founders are different from most businesspeople.

They tend to have problems with boundaries and restrictions. They have a natural inclination to break rules, prove people wrong, and do something that can't be done. They see what others don't see. They take issue with anything that they perceive as inhibiting their creativity and independence. They are comfortable with high levels of ambiguity. They are fine flying a plane with an engine on fire. Propelled by near-delusional levels of self-confidence, they simply *will* stuff to happen.

In the early "knife-fight" stages of a startup's existence, a founder *needs to be weird.* They need to be driven. They need to be relentless, or they won't survive. Picture dozens of freshly hatched sea turtles emerging from the sand and racing toward the ocean, with hundreds of seagulls wheeling overhead. Most of them aren't going to make it. It's the aggressive, semi-delusional founders that reach the ocean. Because of these people, many of us now live in a frictionless world of near-instant communication, retail, and transportation.

But rest assured—at some point, things will start to fall apart. The organization will outpace the individual. The founder will reach the ceiling of their capacity to lead, and all those inspiring knife-fight attributes will suddenly turn problematic. The time bomb will detonate: tick, tick, boom.

Why? Because the same people who command respect and effort also happen to be control freaks who are terrible at delegating and worse at empowering. The same people who will new things into existence are undisciplined workaholics who exhaust themselves and everyone around them. The same people who innovate and inspire frequently lack the EQ to communicate effectively, work through others, and sustain trust. They can see the future, but they lack the capacity to think and organize collectively. They are not your calm, deliberate, and empathetic Tim Cook types. They can charm you with their drive, but they are typically not "fun hangs."

The VCs know this perfectly well. The old model worked like this: They funded these sharp, young founders under the assumption that they would eventually flame out and get replaced by experienced executives. Once the startup gained traction (the thinking went), they would need more disciplined, experienced leadership in order to handle the cascade of organizational challenges that come with rampant growth.

So at some point, they defenestrated the founder and brought in the professional manager (this was the Sequoia Capital formula). The problem, of course, is that the professionals inevitably wound up killing the magic—witness John Sculley's tenure at Apple, for example. To a seasoned COO type, innovation can often look like risk, hazard, and waste. And so they turned previously dynamic companies (that were admittedly organizational basket cases) into orderly zombies.

But then a new wave of founders showed that they could grow with their organization. This was better for everyone. These companies kept their spark, the thing that made them unique. They continued to explore and innovate, not simply manage and maintain. Like Microsoft and Apple before them, their founders avoided the time bomb trap. They defied the conventional wisdom that the same aptitudes required to make an early-stage startup successful—a bias for action, a penchant for risk—would invariably blow it up.

But why should we care? As much attention as it gets, the technology industry only represents about 8% of the US GDP. Has the technology industry helped this country's income equality problem, or has it divided us into haves and have-nots? If the VCs that support it had to choose between fostering genuine innovation and making lots of money, which option do you think they would favor? Have they helped or hurt the industry's "bro culture" problem by applying roughly 3% of their total venture capital toward solo female founders? Is it a bad thing when companies like Theranos and FTX and WeWork fail, taking down all their employees and investors with them?

We should care. Here's why.

The Stakes Are Extremely High

In *2001: A Space Odyssey*, we see the most famous edit in film history: a bone that is used to kill an enemy (and also solve a protein problem) is instantly transformed into a vessel that can explore the universe. Our technology is neutral. Our story is up to us.

The rapid growth of technology over the past couple of hundred years has seen an astonishing amount of progress in living standards, from antibiotics to electricity to education. Technology has enabled the most significant (if underreported) story of our time: more than a billion people have been lifted out of extreme poverty since 1990.

In a *Fortune* piece titled "Fortune's New Global 500 List Shows Europe's Decline, the U.S.'s Rise," Jean-Pascal Tricoire, the then CEO of Schneider Electric, said "the new Fortune Global 500 is 'the reality check . . . of a new world,' in which companies focused on technology and emerging economies have consolidated their global position. While the U.S. and China each saw the rise of Big Tech companies, no European or Japanese tech companies made a similar leap forward."[8]

Human innovation will become *more important*, not less. Speculation will be essential. We are still going to need to place big bets on odd ideas. We're still going to need to fund visionary misfits. But we also need to turn those misfits into responsible leaders. If we can develop founders who can mature as people as their startups mature as companies, to stay responsible and marshal their resources, then we will be able to both (a) solve big problems and (b) improve people's lives.

Surviving founders are still rarely seen in the wild. But the impact of those who have "gone the distance"—Jobs, Zuckerberg, Gates, Benioff, Ellison, Musk—has been meteoric. For every Apple, there are a hundred WeWorks. So, how do we create more durable founders? Especially ones who don't fit the classic tech bro stereotype? How do we push more across the line?

How do we turn founders into keepers?

Defusing the Time Bomb

Dear founders, it's a difficult truth: to grow your startup, you have to grow as a person.

Spend some time with any VC, and they'll tell you the same story: founders tell themselves they will beat the odds, but sooner or later growth catches up with them. You can outrun your limitations for only so long. You must learn how to work through others, not just yourself. It happened with Rich, and it happened with Tien. Outside of some war stories from their peers and a few Peter Drucker quotes, neither of them had good models of leadership to turn toward.

But Rich's research allows founders to build an early warning system to counterbalance the "autopilot" tendencies that can undermine their success. It makes them aware of the pernicious cloud of mental biases that lead them to make terrible decisions that can destroy their company. It helps them see themselves.

This is the goal of this book: to translate Rich's empirical research on leadership in order to understand the psyche of "Homo founderus" and create a road map for developing from a shaky proposition to a solid foundation. To give founders a formal process for effective decision-making, delegating, and team building. To give them (and their investors) the tools they need to defuse the time bomb.

In part one, we'll examine the strengths and weaknesses of founders as a whole, particularly in relation to their corporate executive counterparts. In part two, we'll explore the key differences between successful and unsuccessful founders: Why do some go all the way, while others blow up? And in part three, we'll detail the core competencies that represent the biggest differences between the expectations of stakeholders and the actual performance of founders. In other words, the skills they really need to learn.

But first let's take a look at the fundamentals—the three core competencies that *all* leaders need to succeed.

PART I

Founders, Keepers

CHAPTER 1

The Three Pillars of Leadership

In 1979, Rich left academia and came to Silicon Valley to work for a firm of consulting psychologists who vetted potential executives for big Fortune 500 companies. Their approach was fairly straightforward: The firm administered a brief IQ test to a prospective hire, then conducted a two-hour interview, and then made their recommendations. Conclusions were based on the insights that the psychologists could glean from the candidates' answers to interview questions.

At the time, none of the client information was being seriously collected and analyzed. The psychologist would pull half a dozen themes out of an interview and IQ test, then write up a summary using boilerplate sentences. Some of these interviews were insightful, but most people struggled to draw conclusions about complex personality styles and job and company fit. The company wasn't generating any in-depth profiles or objective, data-based conclusions.

Shortly after joining, Rich came up with the idea of using computers to develop psychological profiles based on personality tests in order to automate the writing of assessment reports and also spot patterns and trends in the data. So he took the computer idea to his boss, who promptly responded, "Young man, you are not being a properly deferential apprentice. Just focus on the work you have been assigned." Rich took his advice to heart and quit.

Over the next few years, Rich entered the outplacement business, help-ing executives find new jobs and providing career counseling. He started using more extensive personality testing and 360-degree ratings (reviews from the subject's coworkers and partners) to help them get a new start. This time, however, he took advantage of his new obsession: technology. He began recording all his research into an early database system in order to discover the broader ideas.

Then, one night, it happened. Rich had his eureka moment. He was preparing to meet with a laid-off executive the following morning. Because his desk wasn't big enough, he covered his bed in dot-matrix printouts. The man's personality test showed that he lacked confidence, suffered from extreme anxiety, had trouble tolerating ambiguity, and had tendencies toward perfectionism. Then Rich looked at his 360 scores: His coworkers said he was indecisive, suffered from analysis paralysis, and was prone to outbursts when he was under stress or when people made mistakes.

One test offered insights into the man's inner life, and the other test described his behavior. *They were a complete match.* The combination of the two assessments instantly revealed what might have taken months of therapy sessions. It got right to the heart of the matter. The next day, Rich shared his insights with his stunned but receptive client. The man later wound up running a major utility company.

Over the next few years, Rich continued his research with a TI-99/4A running at 3 MHz, with 16 KB of RAM and 26 KB of ROM, data storage on a cassette, and a primitive statistics program. Then he moved on to the first IBM PC and created the technology that he is still using today. In addi-tion to diagnostic interviews and personality tests, he began using the then unheard-of multi-rater 360 rating methodology that generated an objective assessment of competencies from superiors, peers, and subordinates and mea-sured almost 50 management, leadership, problem-solving, and social skills.

By the late eighties, Rich had developed a sizable database and was cor-relating personality and 360 ratings. His research on leadership and person-ality started with understanding terminated executives, then moved on to the most highly rated leaders, then to CEOs. Why did some succeed while others failed? Over the course of the next several decades, Rich went on to conduct personality and behavioral profiles on hundreds of executives.

Here is what he discovered.

The Three Pillars of Leadership

Defining truly successful leadership has always been an ongoing debate. In the 1980s Tom Peters and Robert Waterman, in their best-selling book, *In Search of Excellence,* noted that great leaders are primarily defined by a simple and compelling vision. In the 1990s, Daniel Goleman in his best-selling book *Emotional Intelligence* surfaced the importance of social awareness, collaboration, and empathy. Then, in the early 2000s, Larry Bossidy and Ram Charan in their book *Execution* pointed out that while vision and relationships are important, they don't mean anything without architecture and implementation.

To Rich, this all sounded like the parable of the three blind men describing the same elephant in markedly different ways. Surely, all three competency clusters were equally important. Each had their natural strengths and weaknesses. Strength in one was akin to being left- or right-handed—the dominant hand gets more usage and becomes that much more dominant. If you were execution minded, for example, then of course you would use that dominant hand to lead.

But he needed the data to confirm his hypothesis. By applying factor analysis, a method used to reduce a large number of variables into a smaller number of key factors (much like organizing a heap of laundry into piles of related items), he was able to arrive at a fundamental conclusion: All three were essential. Like gravity, which quietly did its work for several billion years before Newton had his revelation under the apple tree, these three competencies represented timeless principles.

What are the Three Pillars? Quite simply, they are clusters of competencies that Rich has determined (through extensive factor analysis) are essential for leadership. Rarely, however, are all three found in the same individual in equal strengths.

The Visionary Evangelist

A great thinker and visionary. But could not
get shit done to save his own life.
—Anonymous 360 feedback

Do any of the following statements apply to you?

- I am better than most people when it comes to influencing others.
- I prefer work activities that involve creative thinking.
- I enjoy being the center of attention.
- I enjoy stating my opinion in meetings.
- Creative ideas frequently come to me at any time, day or night.
- I tend to see opportunities before I see the challenges and risks.
- I feel destined to accomplish great things in my life.
- I have to admit that I am more talented than others.
- It is natural for me to take charge and assume a leadership role when I see an opportunity or have an exciting idea.
- It is easy for me to generate excitement, enthusiasm, and optimism that motivates people to follow my lead.
- I enjoy challenging the status quo and leading change or pursuing new approaches.
- I love developing a vision of what is possible and developing strategic initiatives to make it happen.
- I have always been a bit of a rebel and a nonconformist.
- I dislike rules, policies, and boundaries that restrict my independence and creativity.

If you find yourself nodding your head at the majority of these statements (even the ones that might sound like titanic narcissism or outright pathology to others), you may be a Visionary Evangelist.

"Visionary" and "Evangelist" are two words that get thrown around a lot in Startupland, but we picked them for a reason. The "Visionary" aspect doesn't simply imply an imaginative mindset, it refers to someone who can create a compelling vision of the future *in which others can picture themselves.* "Evangelist" refers to the Pied Piper aspect of this personality. It's one thing to come up with a great idea, it's quite another to convince and cajole other people into turning that idea into a reality.

These are the people who break through—who make the medical, scientific, and technological discoveries, who spark innovative art forms and religious reforms. Leonardo da Vinci, Ada Lovelace, Albert Einstein, Nina Simone, Steve Jobs, Frank Lloyd Wright, Martin Luther King, Frida Kahlo, Marie Curie, John Lennon, Virginia Woolf, and George Lucas are all Visionary Evangelists.

Visionary Evangelists are typically born as problem children. They are, to put it charitably, not team players. From a young age, they are a relentless menace. Their inquisitive nature and proclivity for exploration sometimes endanger life and limb. In his book *Zero to One*, Peter Thiel notes that many of PayPal's early employees shared a common trait—as adolescents they all enjoyed experimenting with explosives.

Visionary Evangelists are exciting. They thrive in the midst of creative destruction. Said one 360 reviewer of their founder: "I witnessed her coming in and ripping apart a process that was outdated, inefficient, and meaningless. It was a beautiful thing." They have a poorly developed sense of fear and no concept of the odds against them. They make the impossible happen. Commented another reviewer: "She always asks why and how to do things differently than have been done. She challenges all legal, regulatory, and financial thought processes and always makes sure we get the best possible answer for the company."

Steve Jobs fit the personality of a Visionary Evangelist perfectly. He had very confident assumptions about how to improve things and solve problems, and he was often correct about those assumptions. He inspired everyone around him. He famously "played the orchestra." He rallied his employees to create a dent in the universe. He was better than everyone else, and he knew it.

He could also be a huge asshole to work with. Andrea "Andy" Cunningham helped launch Apple's original Macintosh. In an interview with *Business Insider*, she had this to say about her experience working with Steve Jobs:

Steve got angry with everybody who worked with him. He was very impatient. He had a vision of what it was that you were supposed to be accomplishing and if you didn't do it fast enough or you didn't do it right enough, he definitely got angry. He threw things at people, nothing heavy, but he threw wads of paper at people, swore at people, and criticized their clothing. He did all those things. So what it did to certain people is it caused us to push even harder and try to be even better, but for some people it destroyed them. Fortunately for me, I was one of the first types and I am forever grateful to him actually for the experience because now I am so much better at what I do than I would have been without him.[1]

While we can't excuse this behavior, we can attempt to explain it: As Cunningham indicates, Jobs was frustrated that *other people weren't seeing the same things he was seeing.* The problem, of course, was that those things existed primarily in his head, and he wasn't doing a very good job at communicating them. This brings us to another key VE characteristic: a propensity for "drive-by delegation." By that, we mean a poorly described assignment that needed to happen yesterday.

Visionary Evangelists are magpies; they tend to get distracted by shiny objects. Fiercely intelligent, they are quickly bored by routine. Systems and processes hold very little appeal—too restrictive, too rote, too many details. As a result, they are much better at launching a project than maintaining, managing, or even sustaining a modicum of interest. One person's relentless curiosity and unceasing inspiration is another person's complete lack of executive functionality: "He loves new and trendy things. That's fine, but it may cause him to miss the value in the tested models."

Visionary Evangelists embody a lot of fascinating contradictions. They are aggressive entrepreneurs who are often deathly afraid of conflict. They are inspirational speakers who are frequently disasters at small talk. Lots of them come from good schools, but they can't concentrate. Some of them wind up leading huge organizations, but they are essentially outcasts and loners. The best of them recognize their weaknesses and put in the hard, unglamorous work of fixing them: learning to be a better listener, making an effort to reply to emails, getting to meetings on time, sticking to deadlines, offering legitimately constructive criticism.

They are notoriously terrible at the mundane but crucial aspects of running a business. Details? Boring. Processes? Stifling. Execution? Someone else's problem. This is why so many startups led by visionary founders stumble when it's time to scale. They are brilliant at sparking the flame but terrible at keeping the fire burning. They understand *their* vision and are confident that they can work their way toward realizing it, and so naturally they assume that other people will get it as well. The end result? Flying wads of paper.

But they are essential. In his book *Notes on Complexity*, Neil Theise, a professor of pathology at the NYU Grossman School of Medicine, discusses the concept of *quenched disorder*, or the necessary "Goldilocks" amount of randomness that all systems need in order to adapt and thrive: "New opportunities can't be found if random things aren't happening here and there, stumbling into new ways of being, new modes to be reconnoitered and exploited. A little randomness keeps the system alive."[2]

Visionary Evangelists provide that randomness, that flickering spark.

The Relationship Builder

Wanting to please everyone all the time sometimes just isn't possible.
—Anonymous 360 feedback

We all want to be nice, but let's face it, some of us are nicer than others. How many of these statements apply to you?

- I find it easy to manage reluctant or uncooperative employees to become committed team members.
- I get a great deal of satisfaction when I am helping an employee who is struggling.
- I try to be positive and patient and avoid upsetting others.
- It is easy for me to get very involved in helping my friends and coworkers with their problems.
- I would genuinely enjoy being a mentor to a student or intern.

- I am quite comfortable openly discussing feelings with my coworkers.
- Compared to my coworkers, I am known as a very caring and supportive boss.
- I have a reputation for being very sensitive to employees' feelings, needs, and concerns.
- I try to bring out the best in people by giving frequent praise, recognition, and support.
- My coworkers see me as a friendly and approachable person.
- My ability to read people and understand their motivations and needs is better than most of my coworkers.
- I am good at getting people to like me.
- Building strong relationships with my colleagues is very important to me.
- I have been told that I am too nice and do not demand enough performance from people.

If you're the kind of person who actually *enjoys* team offsites, likes to talk on the phone just to talk on the phone, and sends people texts on their birthdays, you may be a Relationship Builder. And this cold, cruel world needs more people like you.

Relationship Builders are genuinely positive people. They are welcoming, approachable, and nonjudgmental. They tend to see the best in others and treat everyone with respect and consideration. "He is very easy-going and approachable," a direct report said. "He has a warm and friendly personality and is instantly liked. I can't think of anybody who doesn't like him."

Some public examples of leaders who are Relationship Builders include people like Howard Schultz, Indra Nooyi, Oprah Winfrey, Barack Obama, and Richard Branson. To quote Mahatma Gandhi: "I suppose leadership at one time meant muscles; but today, it means getting along with people."

Consider Satya Nadella, CEO of Microsoft, who transformed the company's culture by emphasizing empathy, collaboration, and a growth mindset. Under his leadership, Microsoft has shifted from a cutthroat,

Darwinian environment to a place where teamwork and inclusivity are prioritized. Another great example of a Relationship Builder is Tony Hsieh, the late CEO of Zappos. Hsieh was known for his extraordinary emphasis on company culture and employee happiness, which he believed were key to the success of the business. His leadership style was built on trust, open communication, and fostering strong relationships within the organization.

Here's the basic Relationship Builder perspective: The world is generally a safe place, and most people are basically good and can be trusted. Considering the fact that we spend almost half our lives working in the company of people who are essentially strangers, this kind of empathetic attitude can go a long way. It earns them the respect and trust of others: "In my experience, in direct relationships, she has never been anything but open, friendly, and approachable," one executive said of his colleague. "She extends trust in all her interactions, and therefore usually receives it."

Relationship Builders are what we call in our research a *model of values*—they have high moral and ethical standards and consistently try to live up to them. Their behavior reflects their principles. They try to be just and fair, including the willingness to take responsibility for their mistakes rather than blaming others when things go wrong. They emphasize treating people with respect. They take the Boy and Girl Scout stuff seriously. It matters to them. They are the happy warriors, the people you want on your side when things get tough.

Relationship builders are also *socially astute*: They know how to read a room. They are canny diplomats who are quick to adjust their approach to fit another person's mood or need. They can quickly intuit the social dynamics of working groups. They listen attentively and don't interrupt. They remain calm and unflappable when the meeting gets testy.

In a bleak transactional world, where opportunists flit from company to company like butterflies, Relationship Builders are invaluable because they build the ties that bind. They are the cultural glue. They get people invested. They foster ownership. They develop a sense of shared fate, the feeling that "we're all in this together." They make people feel 10 feet tall, willing to rise to any challenge, endure hardships, and make personal sacrifices (such as working long hours when necessary or accepting deferred financial rewards) for the cause. Remember, this is all an exercise in collective imagination.

This brings us to the central paradox of the Relationship Builder: *They are conflict resolvers who hate conflict.* These people are brilliant at facilitating dialogue. They are the ones sitting in the middle chair of the group circle. But because they are so sensitive to other people's feelings and are driven by a need to be liked by everyone, they don't like to deliver bad news or be directly involved in conflict and disharmony. When they find themselves in a really nasty dustup (particularly one involving themselves), they either paper it over or avoid it altogether: "It feels like he really wants to avoid confrontation and have other people make the decisions, and he seems particularly uncomfortable handling the issues with the EVPs."

But it's a fact of startup life: Shit happens. All teams have moments of distrust and disunity, especially when they feel stuck and frustrated. People point fingers, blame others, and revert to their petulant adolescent selves. There is nothing a typical Relationship Builder would like more than to avoid conflicts like this. But the leader who fails to address conflict directly is setting the stage for hypocrisy, secrecy, cliques, backstabbing, and all manner of palace intrigue that poisons the atmosphere and undermines productivity: "She has too many people she has to try to please. She can sometimes get caught up in that and lose sight of our objectives. I've been asked to do things at times that are not worth my time or effort just because someone on the outside 'thinks' it should be done or for the 'dog and pony show' of it."

Their deep empathy and desire to avoid conflict can make them indecisive and overly accommodating. They may struggle with holding people accountable, fearing that tough love might damage relationships. In the pressure cooker of startup life, this can lead to a lack of discipline and accountability that undermines the entire organization. They can be so focused on keeping everyone happy that they lose sight of the bigger picture, becoming reluctant to make the hard decisions that leadership sometimes demands. In short, they can be too nice for their own good.

But they remain indispensable. Relationship Builders bring compassion and humanity to business. They weave the social fabric of the organization. They may not have visionary zeal or managerial rigor, but they are essential ingredients in the mix that makes a successful company. Without a Relationship Builder in an active leadership role, a startup can be a desolate place to work, driven by a checked-out Visionary Evangelist who likes ideas more than people, or a process-obsessed Manager of Execution who lives entirely inside spreadsheets.

Relationship Builders remind us that we are human and that we don't have all the answers.

The Manager of Execution

There are days when I'm glad that I work with him, not for him.
—Anonymous 360 feedback

Finally, do any of these statements apply to you? Be honest:

- I like to have things under control by having a plan, and I rarely, if ever, do anything reckless or impulsive.
- When I go into a new initiative or project, I prefer to reduce uncertainty by trying to find out as much as I can about what I can expect or how things might turn out.
- Compared to my colleagues, I am much more focused on planning, goal setting, and monitoring performance.
- I have a reputation for being a pragmatic realist who makes fact-based, rational decisions.
- When I use a tool or object, I always put it back where I got it.
- I like making lists of all of the things I have to do.
- I am quite comfortable with a certain amount of routine and regular in my habits.
- I have a reputation for holding people accountable and for having a low tolerance for substandard performance.

- I am a very good project manager. I get things done in a focused, systematic, and efficient manner.
- I have little trouble making tough decisions about employees who are not performing.
- I pride myself in meeting commitments and delivering on time and on budget.
- I am good at bringing order and focus to projects and organizations.
- I feel a sense of responsibility to set high standards of performance and expect excellence from myself and others.
- I believe that this generation would be better off if those in authority were shown more respect.

If you're the kind of person who checks their grocery receipts in the car, genuinely enjoys home maintenance, schedules regular community service appointments, and likes to spend your free time organizing, you may be a Manager of Execution. And you are absolutely essential.

Vision without execution is hallucination. If you don't have people who finish what they start and make sure that others do the same, you will have problems. Meetings won't begin on time. Projects will limp along until they evaporate entirely. Pie-in-the-sky quarterly goals will be dismissed out of hand. And none of it will matter, because no one will be held accountable. Even with the best of intentions and an inspirational vision, without a Manager of Execution, you're sunk. Public examples of Managers of Execution include people like Steve Kerr, Tiger Woods, Lou Gerstner, Meg Whitman, and Michael Dell.

Managers of Execution deliver results. Their orientation is toward focus and efficiency. Their graph always goes up and to the right. They provide clarity and direction. They turn the hazy dream into a sharp reality. You can almost hear the martial drums beating as we describe them. They understand that work without focus is fatal.

Take Mary Barra, CEO of General Motors. Barra's focus on execution and operational excellence has driven GM through a significant transformation, including the aggressive push toward electric vehicles. Another example is Tim Cook. While Jobs was the quintessential Visionary Evangelist,

Cook is the epitome of a Manager of Execution. His meticulous attention to supply chain management and operational efficiency has allowed Apple to maintain its status as one of the most valuable companies in the world, even after the passing of its iconic founder.

Managers of Execution have a strict set of personal values and a sense of responsibility. They have a strong inner compass. In a conversation, you might hear a Manager of Execution say, "My values may seem to be a little old-fashioned by modern standards." They hold themselves to their commitments, and they expect others to do the same. Ethics and work are one and the same: "Dependable, reliable, honest, hardworking, and driven . . . he loves to solve problems. He manages both his time and the time and energy of his staff with effective direction and guidance."

While they like nothing better than to sequester themselves with a spreadsheet, the best of them understand that process is about efficiency. They know that margins make the difference. So they stay focused on organizational goals and are rarely distracted or set off course by unimportant details or activities: "She and her team understand that we are all working for the same goals: satisfied customers and profitable business decisions. They make business decisions with sensitivity to customer need."

Startups *need* Managers of Execution in order to scale effectively. Without them, they will run out of cash, overhire, overcommit to customer requests, or similarly self-destruct in a whirlwind of activity that is completely lacking in actual productivity. The company will either limp along in endless circles or flame out like a supernova. Managers of Execution help them set priorities and understand the organization's real capabilities.

Unfortunately, this gets harder to do as bureaucracy develops. Work creates more work: more dependencies, more meetings, more action items. Organizations generate useless activity like the sun generates solar flares. All too often, this kind of environment can feed a Manager of Execution's worst impulses. To quote Jeff Bezos:

> Good process serves you so you can serve customers. But if you're not watchful, the process can become the thing. This can happen very easily in large organizations. The process becomes the proxy

for the result you want. You stop looking at outcomes and just make sure you're doing the process right. Gulp. It's not that rare to hear a junior leader defend a bad outcome with something like, "Well, we followed the process." A more experienced leader will use it as an opportunity to investigate and improve the process. The process is not the thing. It's always worth asking, do we own the process or does the process own us?[3]

What happens when Managers of Execution fall prey to their worst impulses and get lost in the process? All sorts of grimly predictable stuff. The sad truth of the matter is that most businesses encourage and promote people with obsessive-compulsive tendencies who are driven to be in control of their circumstances down to the last detail. The end result? These people briskly and efficiently navigate their companies to the bottom of the ocean.

They micromanage. These folks like to be in control. Rather than leveraging the energy and talent of others—a critical leadership skill—they often feel they don't have time to involve others, to tell or show them what needs to be done. They have very little predisposition for dealing with actual, living, breathing human beings. They would much prefer to turn the organization into a smoothly functioning machine: "He needs to work on his interpersonal skills. He does not listen patiently or respectfully and tries to take charge of areas that organizationally belong to others. Sometimes I think he also withholds information as a way to retain control." Yikes.

They often suffer from "engineer's disease"—because they are experts in a certain financial or technical discipline, they are therefore experts in *everything*: "She can be insensitive, overly assertive, and at times overbearing. Because of these traits, people may not always give her the complete picture or tell her what is really on their minds. These traits detract from her aligning the organization behind her goals and building trust among key employees." Here's a quote from Kurt Vonnegut's 1952 novel *Player Piano* that neatly sums up the problem:

"If only it weren't for the people, the goddamned people," said Finnerty, "always getting tangled up in the machinery. If it weren't for them, the earth would be an engineer's paradise."[4]

Managers of Execution can easily fail forward. They can rise through the ranks, while the people who have the misfortune to work for them stay miserable. But they will fail to create strong teams, delegate effectively, or build an enduring organization. They build dungeons and trapdoors, not castles and bridges. We all know what these kinds of zombie companies are like, limping along as moderately profitable mediocrities. When the politics and the palace intrigue become more important than the actual results (not that anyone would admit that), the smart talent jumps ship.

But at the end of the day, we need Managers of Execution—preferably ones who also happen to be balanced human beings.

Why All Three Pillars Matter

The Visionary Evangelist, the Relationship Builder, and the Manager of Execution are all essential to the success of any organization, but each brings unique strengths and corresponding weaknesses. An organization led solely by a Visionary Evangelist may blaze bright but burn out quickly, undone by its inability to execute. A company dominated by Relationship Builders may be a great place to work but could falter without a clear vision or the discipline to deliver results. And a firm run by Managers of Execution may be efficient but soulless, marching toward mediocrity rather than greatness.

Each contributes to a cycle of leadership that is essential to any startup: setting direction, inspiring others to follow, and delivering results. But the message is clear: to be an effective founder, *you have to be good at lots of things.*

The Three Pillars of Leadership

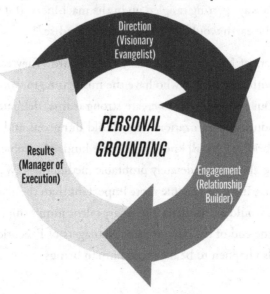

Manager of Execution Competencies:
1. Decisiveness
2. Holding people accountable
3. Dependability
4. Developing structures, systems, and processes
5. Reengineering processes
6. Emphasizing excellence
7. Results and productivity

Visionary Evangelist Competencies:
1. Inspirational role model
2. Agent of change
3. Taking initiative
4. External focus
5. Visionary thinking
6. Strategic focus
7. Model of commitment

8. Self-confidence
9. Creating meaning

Relationship Builder Competencies:

1. Building teams
2. Creating buy-in
3. Adaptability
4. Building partnerships
5. Social astuteness
6. Model of values
7. Relationship building
8. Facilitating conflict resolution
9. Handling resistance to change

This is why the most successful organizations are those that cultivate all three pillars. It's about balance. A great company needs the visionary spark to inspire, the relational glue to bind, and the operational rigor to execute. Each pillar supports the others, compensating for their weaknesses and amplifying their strengths.

The Founder's Dilemma

For most of the twentieth century, learning how to lead a large organization entailed working at one: IBM, Johnson & Johnson, General Motors, etc. Executives worked at these companies for decades to gain the tools they needed so they could (a) set direction, (b) bind talent, and (c) deliver results. As a result, the ones who made it to the top were fairly well-rounded. At the very least, they were ambidextrous—adept at switching competencies.

In a large organization, it's not enough to be a visionary or a people person or an operational expert—you need to be all three, or at least understand how to lead a team that embodies all three capacities. For a long time, Rich enjoyed a very fulfilling career helping these kinds of executives climb their way to the top of the ladder.

Then he met Tien.

The venture capitalist Peter Fenton said to Rich: "Hey, I just came out of a board meeting, and we have this founder who sure could use some help. Will you meet him?" After spending time with Tien, Rich realized he was dealing with an altogether different kind of beast. This particular executive was far from well-rounded, but then again, how could he be? He didn't have 30 years of working at HP under his belt. Then again, he wouldn't have lasted three years at HP. It would have driven him into lunacy.

What's more, there were lots of people out there like Tien. These were very different people from Rich's old clients. They didn't wear suits. They didn't play golf. They weren't the most gifted public speakers. Many of them appeared to be downright asocial. Some of their companies, however, grew to become tremendously successful. Despite their flaws (or perhaps because of them?), people seemed to genuinely admire these people. But they clearly needed some coaching.

These "founders" simply didn't have the big company training. For many of them, this was their first job out of school. They skewed heavily toward Visionary Evangelists, which wasn't much of a surprise. They generally didn't have much to offer other than an informed idea. They generally sucked at relationships and execution, because vision was their dominant hand. It wasn't their fault. They simply didn't know what they didn't know.

This odd-duck profile fascinated Rich. It was as if he had discovered a new species in the wild. And for the rest of his career, he chose to focus almost exclusively on founders: what makes them tick, what makes them different, and most importantly, why most fail but a few manage to succeed. Here's what he learned, starting with what makes a founder a founder.

CHAPTER 2

What Makes a Founder a Founder?

What makes a founder a founder? Is it how well you did in school or which one you attended? How young or old you are? How much professional experience you've gathered over the years? Does it concern your technical background (or lack thereof)? What's more important when defining a founder: biography or personality?

Some Common Myths

Let's start with biography. There are two stereotypical images of founders: the Ivy League dropout who launches out of a prominent accelerator program to storm the market with a crazy new idea, or the middle-aged MBA with a massive network who leaves a top-tier software company to tackle an obscure enterprise problem. Neither, of course, is entirely accurate. There is no such thing as a typical founder profile. But both are stereotypes for a reason.

Thanks to the recent research of entrepreneurs and academics like Ali Tamaseb and Pierre Azoulay,[1] we can dispel lots of common myths about founders. Let's start with age. The *median* age of successful founders is in the mid-30s, meaning half are younger and half are older. Bill Porter founded E-Trade when he was 54. Aaron Levie dropped out of his junior year at USC to start Box. Experience counts for a lot, until it doesn't.

Let's look at education. More founders hold advanced degrees than dropped out of college, but neither factor materially influenced their chance of success. As many of them attended Ivy League–type institutions as those who went to schools that didn't rank in the top one hundred. And as it turns out, you don't have to know how to code. Roughly half of successful founders are nontechnical.

What about their entrepreneurial ideas? Frustrations from personal experience inspire some "mission-driven" founders—Dropbox founder Drew Houston famously left his homework on a thumb drive in his dorm room at MIT, for example. Canva's Melanie Perkins was frustrated with the cost and complication of available graphic design tools. However, just as many chose the "mercenary" approach: pick a growing market trend and then identify a significant problem. Also, there's no disadvantage to being a solo founder versus being in the classic "tech savvy/business savvy" partnership.

So much for broad generalizations! The only definitive biographical observation we can make about all founders is that (a) they are overwhelmingly male and (b) they overwhelmingly fail. Fortunately, many more female founders are launching thriving startups, but that 90% failure rate remains stubbornly persistent.

In order to find out what truly makes a founder a founder, we're going to have to look elsewhere. In fact, we think you should throw biography completely out the window.

Personality > Biography

When we look at all of our data, we find that what makes a founder a founder is clearly, irrefutably, their *personality*: their internal psyche and their external behavior. In other words, what's going on in their heads and what their colleagues see them doing. In the grand debate between nature and nurture, when it comes to founders, we are planting our flag on nature. We believe that personality triumphs biography.

Understanding what it takes to be a successful founder entails a deep exploration into the personality and behavioral traits that drive entrepreneurial success. Rich's database, comprising comprehensive personality tests and 360-degree assessments of 122 founders, provides a window into the minds and behaviors of these visionary leaders. By analyzing this rich trove of data, we can uncover the key psychological drivers and capabilities that differentiate the most successful founders from the rest.

The 122 founders in our dataset come from three sources: founders who discovered Rich on the web (via reading about his work or the leadership columns on his blogs), referrals from other founders he has coached, or referrals from venture capitalists. It's important to note that this is obviously not a randomly selected group of all possible founders, which is a limitation of this study.

First, all of these founders took a 327-question personality test, which assessed them on a number of *personality traits* that our research has correlated with effective or ineffective leadership. Some examples of these traits include impulsivity, patience, social adroitness, dominance, responsibility, empathy, and autonomy. The test includes several "trap" questions to ensure that founders aren't overinflating (or underselling) their various traits.

Second, key stakeholders (investors, board members, advisors, direct reports, former colleagues) were asked to rate the founder's performance (on a five-point scale) on 46 separate *leadership competencies* (as opposed to personality traits). Some examples of these competencies include strategic focus, delegation and empowerment, and openness to input (you can find the entire list at the end of this book). Crucially, these stakeholders were also asked to rate how *important* each competency was to the success of the founder's job. The most significant gaps between the performance and importance ratings determined the weaker competencies to address.

Here's some more background on our methodology:

- **How did you determine the three primary leadership competency clusters?** Factor analysis was used to identify broad leadership competency clusters, which we call the Three Pillars of

Leadership (the Visionary Evangelist, the Relationship Builder, and the Manager of Execution), introduced in the previous chapter.

- **How did you determine what constituted a successful founder?** Our founder success metric was derived by measuring their MOIC, or multiple on invested capital. These numbers were provided by Arbor Ventures, who did the research to find a metric that represented the founder's ability to increase shareholder value significantly, irrespective of personal traits. Success was defined by a 10x return on investment. Founders were then put into two groups: those with the 10x returns and an equal number of founders with the lowest returns.

- **How did you determine the differences between financially successful and unsuccessful founders?** Discriminant analysis and stepwise regression were used to identify the significant differences. These competencies encompassed a diverse set of characteristics that historical research has suggested are related to a leader's effectiveness. Their leadership skills, management skills, social skills, decision-making skills, and many other personal characteristics covered a wide range of traits and behaviors. Raters were asked to make quantitative assessments of each skill, offer comments to explain their rating, and also assess the relative importance of each skill to the founder's success.

- **How did you determine the largest "importance versus performance" competency gaps?** The largest gaps were identified based on the ratings of the board and the executives working for the founder on (a) the importance of each skill and (b) the founder's execution of those skills. These competency gaps represent the differences between what the board and the executives expect, and the founder's actual performance.

- **How did you determine the differences between founders and senior executives?** To understand how founders as a group differed from a global sample of other senior executives, 360 ratings and personality traits and patterns were compared with a dataset of 1,500 executives from a global sample of companies of different sizes, industries, and countries. We used this executive dataset to create a normal distribution (i.e., norms of "50" for all of the personality scores and 360 ratings). The comparison of the founder dataset against this normal distribution is the basis of our conclusions.

- **Where did all the feedback comments spread throughout this book come from?** All these comments come from the 360 review process, which typically generates hundreds of comments per founder. As a result, we've been able to take advantage of thousands of anonymous, "on the ground" observations, which we've used to help bring the quantitative data to life. Some of these comments have been edited for clarity and concision.

So there you have it. When we apply all this statistical analysis to our founder dataset, some obvious patterns begin to emerge. Let's start with the good news.

The Good

Almost all founders are strong Visionary Evangelists.

They are *astute observers of external trends*. They have a keen sense of the broader narrative arcs of technology and the market. They are voracious consumers of information.

But they are not simply news addicts. By bouncing ideas off their networks and mining their experiences, they can synthesize all this information into sharp commercial insights. They are naturally curious animals who scan their environmental context to find problems that need solving and better ways to solve them. They can spot the industry inefficiencies and the burning customer needs.

"She's constantly coming up with different approaches," says a colleague of a founder in one of our 360 tests. "Many of her ideas come from reading articles, books, etc., which is contagious for those around her. She's

always wanting to try something new if she thinks it will make us better . . .
it's challenging to keep up but awesome to be a part of."

"He's a marketing machine," says another. "I liken him to 3M, a company that is famous for putting things together in new ways. They didn't
create the sticky note, but they made a much better one. I'm not sure that
he is necessarily the most innovative or creative founder I've worked with in
terms of coming up with a fantastic product or idea, but what he's done is
be able to recognize, 'Hey, this a definite shift that's happening, and I can
see how our competitors are trying things, but it really should be this plus
that.' And he's always right."

After serving as the first CMO of Salesforce, Tien cofounded Zuora in
2008 to address a big problem: Subscription billing for digital companies was
a nightmare, and all the old telco solutions were hopelessly outdated. But this
inefficiency inspired a broader vision: One day all companies will become
subscription companies, meaning they'll need a new financial platform.

"During the early days of Zuora," says Tien, "we would sit often around
a dinner table with a bottle of wine and try to stump ourselves—what can't
you subscribe to?" They couldn't find an answer, and the subscription economy was born.

Founders *challenge the status quo*. That's the ticket to the startup dance.
They question things that most people take for granted. They tend to be
unorthodox thinkers who reject traditional approaches and challenge established boundaries. Their inherent curiosity fuels their insights and helps
them come up with creative solutions that others may have overlooked.
They have a sense of creative antagonism that motivates them to start their
own company in the first place.

"He's catalytic with his mere presence," says a colleague. "He can
see around corners and will challenge the status quo when he envisions a
change will make an improvement. He's willing to let people experiment
with solutions and grants us the autonomy to make drastic changes when
we think it is important. A great example of this was a 'stability mutiny'
day, when we abandoned our regularly scheduled work and focused on a
problem we felt was important."

Founders are *confident risk-takers*. They enjoy taking chances. Startups are the dictionary definition of the term "risky business." They certainly recognize that the odds are long, but their self-confidence compels them to jump in regardless. Founders believe that even when most people have failed to solve a problem, they will come up with a creative solution. They believe that they are destined to do great things in their lives.

Founders are *effective influencers*. They're better than most people when it comes to convincing and inspiring others: employees, investors, and the press. They can motivate their team to work hard and persevere through tough times and convince investors to back their venture. Some founders are optimistic and enthusiastic cheerleaders. Others are simply powerful communicators who paint a compelling vision with passion and clarity. Still others inspire with their determination to succeed and willingness to work hard.

"We put her in front of clients to help close business as much as we could because she was just so charismatic," says a colleague. "She would confidently make these matter-of-fact statements that totally won you over. You'd sit in a room, and she'd tell you the sky is green. By the end of the conversation, you would believe that the sky is green. Or at least you would go outside and check."

Everyone wants to feel part of a bigger story. Founders give their employees a keen sense that they are part of a seismic shift—a new and exciting commercial trend that others have missed. They create a compelling vision of the future that others feel encouraged to inhabit and participate in. They give their teams a "North Star," a clear vision of what is informing their broader strategic decisions. They give everyone a sense that they are part of a broader conversation.

Founders *work incredibly hard*. Running a startup was once memorably compared to "crawling across broken glass." Growing a company requires an intense, sustained effort and a huge amount of commitment. Founders are often consumed with their jobs, think about their company day and night, and put in long hours to make the organization successful.

"The startup is an extension of his being, and so he is amped all the time," says a colleague. "Whereas the regular employee can detach and go home and focus on their family or whatever. They get to leave it behind. That's not the case for him. He has no off button."

A VC once told Rich, "I'm looking for someone who's willing to hit the wall. And hit the wall. And hit the wall. And do it over and over again, until the wall comes down." These people don't get discouraged by problems and obstacles. They are tenacious in pursuing their vision. Work-life balance is nonexistent, and startups are notorious relationship killers. Many people have to learn to adjust as they grow older or start families. That being said, the concept of a "workaholic founder" is redundant.

Founders are also exceptionally good at *handling stress.* In his excellent book *Zero to IPO*, Okta cofounder Frederic Kerrest observes that in standardized psychological profiles, founders have more in common with military commandos and athletes than other business executives.[2] Despite all the havoc they have to endure, they generally receive high marks from their coworkers on resilience and stress management. But stress tends to take its toll. There are lots of ways to take a two-hour vacation.

Finally, founders *take initiative.* They have a bias for action. They can't help it. They are quick to identify new problems or new opportunities. They are forceful, commanding individuals who take charge and get things moving.

The Bad

In the Three Pillars framework, founders are mediocre to average at relationship building.

They generally score lower than average on 360 ratings of *sensitivity, consideration*, and *empathy.* The ones who score particularly low on these ratings are often seen as not particularly considerate, compassionate, or caring. They criticize people in public, which is not just humiliating, it poisons trust: "Those who put out their necks, take chances, are subject to unjust public hangings. This encourages those who are afraid of these consequences, which is most of the team, to either simply align with the founder or keep their heads down. When he is not in meetings, I see cooperation and teamwork."

Founders have *difficulty staying in touch with the pulse of the organization*. They focus most of their attention on achieving their vision, keeping a close eye on competitors, raising investment capital, and recruiting talent. In other words, *everything but their company*. As a result, the workforce often feels like nobody is minding the store.

"A lot of times I get the feeling that I'm listening to a presentation deck that she just gave to some investors," says a colleague. "When she does engage with the organization, it feels really tactical and inauthentic. There's a weird disconnect." Says another colleague: "She doesn't have a good pulse of what's going on in the company. She relies on a few insiders to get a sense of the temperature and only becomes really involved when there's a heightened reactive situation, like when someone is threatening to quit."

Startups are stressful places. Responsibilities are not clearly defined. Border skirmishes over who owns what create political battles. Founders are generally seen by their colleagues as being able to handle this stress fairly well. But what we know from their personality tests is that many are simply very good at hiding the fact that they're stressed. And those who are struggling with unsuccessful businesses often blow up (successful founders can lose it as well, of course). They become reactive and impulsive. It shows itself in criticism, sarcasm, outbursts, avoidance, withdrawal, passive-aggressive resistance, and (when things get really ugly) legal action. They're simply less grounded.

The problem is that founders *generally have an IQ much higher than their EQ*. They are happy to engage in discursive chat, but they are simply not comfortable with the emotions generated by conflicts and tough conversations. At the same time, they are impatient, outspoken, and demanding and are often the source of conflicts or simply make them worse.

So, what happens when conflict happens? The majority try to ignore it or sweep it under the rug. They tell themselves that their team members are adults and should be able to resolve their conflicts on their own. Sometimes, they believe they should just sit like a judge in court and decide who wins and who loses. That rarely works: the conflicts linger, the resentments grow.

"He more often than not increases conflict. He optimizes for people liking him rather than getting a resolution that is optimized for the company."

"She does not like conflicts. Often she either gets angry and demands her way, or runs away from the problem without resolution."

"It seems whenever there is a major conflict, the other person just ends up fired, but nobody is ever fired for poor performance."

Finally, founders have *difficulty delegating and empowering people*. They are control freaks who won't let go. They make too many unilateral decisions, which can become human roadblocks and slow down the organization. Their natural tendency is to go off to the mountain, talk to God, and come down with the tablets. They need to make the transition to a different view of their role, as the facilitator of teamwork. This attitude can't be faked: "He has to stop using the pronoun 'I' all the time. He is quick to point out areas where improvement can be found, and very slow to compliment."

Secretly, many founders genuinely don't really like group meetings and have little tolerance for open disagreement with their ideas. After all, in the past, they've done their most creative and productive work by themselves. They are skeptical about whether group problem-solving or strategic planning will add value. They get so focused on what they are trying to accomplish that they don't see how their behavior may hurt feelings or intimidate people. Social astuteness and working through others is not their strong suit.

The Worse

Finally, within the Three Pillars framework, founders are utterly dismal Managers of Execution.

Founders have *difficulty providing focus*, because you can't share what you don't have. They are perpetually fascinated by new ideas and new opportunities. They are magpies who chase after bright shiny things. So they drive everyone around them crazy. Everything is chaos: an endless stream of fits and pivots. Every new feature, new marketing plan, reorganization, or strategic shift takes its toll.

"He is not a process person," says one colleague. "He doesn't run meetings in an organized fashion, doesn't recap the action items and owners, doesn't hold himself to the road map, distracts the plan with all sorts of ad hoc projects. He can often be found looking at his phone when he is bored."

Startups have to be agile, but agility requires actionable solutions that have clear priorities. The problem is that (particularly when they don't work out) those priorities tend to get lost in the startup flux. How many startup companies spend as much time learning from their failures as celebrating their successes?

"Operationally, he's a disaster," says a colleague. "Put simply: we have never established short- or medium-term goals. Milestones don't exist. We often get distracted by unimportant details as a result. It's a clusterfuck. We're doing a bit better, but it's extremely important that people understand not just where we're going in five years, but where we're going in the next six months, and how we're going to get there."

Founders are *allergic to scaling*. They are quick to reward people for all-nighters and heroic efforts rather than encouraging people to develop systems and processes to avoid the last-minute shit shows that prompted these efforts. You might stumble into net growth without the processes in place to handle increased complexity, but you won't be efficient about it: "At the end of a 12-hour day, we had to ask him to stop cleaning up the office every night," says a colleague. "We suggested that he could make better use of his time."

"If he just let us do this, we'd be better off," says a colleague about their founder's congenital inability to provide structure. "He's so obviously incapable of establishing effective systems/processes that he should really leave this to others. There's plenty of experience on the team to do this effectively on our own. However, he not only doesn't contribute in this area, but actually impedes our ability to improve our processes by questioning our decisions or saying he wants to do it himself and that we're not allowed to do it, and then dropping the ball."

Lots of founders ultimately miss the old days, when everyone did everything. They pine for the lean months, the war stories, the near misses, and the scrappy triumphs. But this way of doing things simply doesn't scale: "Products are shipped at a slower rate than our competitors in part because he is often a roadblock," says a colleague. "Frequently I'll ask about the status of a new feature and hear, 'Waiting on him to approve.' This seems like a hurdle to scaling and keeping up with the competition. Also, he does get distracted by things that don't matter that much, like Twitter or Hacker News."

Again: "With 20/20 hindsight he should have dug in more and seen the signs that things were not on track. It's unclear what he values. He sometimes appears to favor the dramatic fire drills and the last-minute catches versus the people who quietly deliver time after time with no drama."

Founders tend to have *very high expectations*. What they don't realize is that expectations without clear and specific goals are just attitudes: "Often dismissive of ideas to improve team structure and focus. Demands to insert himself in all structures and systems, even though his functional utility in those systems is zero." Here's another jaw-dropper: "I suspect most people in the company have only a vague idea of what goals they are expected to meet."

Founders are *terrible at giving praise and recognition*. They're equally abysmal at coaching. They tend to throw people into the deep end and expect them to figure out how to swim. What feedback they do manage to offer is often contaminated by frustration and anger. It frequently takes the form of a rant.

"This happens basically never," says one colleague regarding founder praise. "When it does happen (e.g., he'll call someone out during wins), it seems inauthentic. I think because it's so infrequent and the forum is always the same. He could easily throw out more 'Nice job!' and 'Great stuff!' in person and over written communication on a day-to-day basis, but for some reason doesn't."

■ ■ ■

So there you have it: the good, the bad, and the worse. All founders are a mixture of positives and negatives. There are no heroes or villains in this story. The same innate strengths you possess as a founder—creativity, independence, tenacity, intelligence—have a darker side: distractibility, condescension, egotism, and aloofness. The task at hand is to identify those dark-side tendencies and ameliorate them.

When it comes to founder weaknesses, you're not trying to get from good to great. You're trying to get from terrible to average.

PART II

The Differences Between Successful and Unsuccessful Founders

CHAPTER 3

The Myth of the Genius Jerk

Little else mattered so long as WeWork's shares were going up in value . . . Now, though, [Neumann's] magic was gone. He was no longer a visionary able to move mountains. He was a meme—a caricature of an irresponsible CEO, driven by avarice and narcissism. Now that the public market investors had made clear they didn't think WeWork was even a $15 billion or a $20 billion company, it was obvious the billions on paper had vanished. Neumann's power—his invincibility—plunged with it.

So the knives came out.

—Eliot Brown and Maureen Farrell, *The Cult of We: WeWork, Adam Neumann, and the Great Startup Delusion*[1]

The Steve Jobs Question

Narcissism is a personality disorder characterized by grandiosity, a constant need for attention, and a lack of empathy, which can devolve into cruel and manipulative behavior. The narcissist is a familiar character; we've all had the misfortune to encounter these people. We see them on television all the time. But this begs a question: Aren't all founders a bit narcissistic?

Of course they are. A heightened sense of self-worth is fundamental to their identity. We depend upon these people to raise funds, generate attention, attract talent, build dreams, and conquer the market. Perhaps most importantly, they need to believe in themselves amid a cascade of daily failures and whispered aspersions. But when self-confidence slips into narcissism, then trouble ensues.

Narcissists prioritize their own ideas, severely limiting their capacity to learn and adapt. They are terrible at working through others. Their transactional view of relationships is utterly corrosive to trust and loyalty within the team. While risk-taking is a part of startup culture, a narcissist's overconfidence and unchecked ego results in impulsive decisions that frequently detonate in their face. They bend rules, and when they get away with it, they do it at greater and greater scale. A *New York Times* piece called "The End of Faking It in Silicon Valley" notes that in a tighter market, VC firms are becoming increasingly wary of "Machiavellian narcissist" founders:

> When start-up valuations were soaring, [venture capitalists] were seen as visionary kingmakers. It was easy enough to convince the world and the investors in their funds—pension funds, college endowments, and wealthy individuals—that they were responsible stewards of capital with the unique skills required to predict the future and find the next Steve Jobs to build it. But as more start-up frauds are revealed, these titans of industry are playing a different role in lawsuits, bankruptcy filings, and court testimonies: the victim that got duped.[2]

Ultimately, narcissistic founders simply don't know who they are. Externally they project superiority, but internally they are riven with anxiety. They are playing a role tailored to impress their audience. They have no true sense of self.

Here's a question that's probably on your mind at this point: If narcissistic blowhards make such poor leaders, then why do some of the most titanically successful people on the planet happen to be narcissistic blowhards?

We all know the stories. Steve Jobs threatening to fire an entire elevator's worth of employees if they couldn't articulate what they were working on and how it benefited Apple. Elon Musk firing engineers on the spot. Jeff Bezos creating a work culture characterized by people crying inside their cubicles. Larry Ellison endorsing a biography suggesting that the difference between God and him is "God doesn't think he's Larry Ellison."[3]

The conventional wisdom is that to be a successful founder, you also need to be an obsessive egomaniac. Not only is this wrong, it's poisonous, and it's created a generation of founders who have created toxic work environments. Over the years, corporate boards have sent Rich a parade of leaders cursed with this delusion. To quote Netflix cofounder Reed Hastings: "Some companies tolerate [brilliant jerks]. For us, the cost to effective teamwork is too high."[4]

Here's why the conventional wisdom is wrong.

First, correlation does not imply causation. Just because someone achieved success while behaving poorly doesn't mean their bad behavior caused their success. Attributing achievements solely to tyrannical tendencies is both simplistic and misleading.

Second, survivorship bias skews our perception. We tend to concentrate on people who passed a selection process while overlooking those who did not. Let's not forget the countless founders who adopted jerk-like behaviors and failed miserably. May they rest in peace.

Third, these people also benefit from availability bias, or the tendency to overgeneralize based on a handful of very public examples. The media loves the "genius jerk" archetype because drama and conflict sell stories. Most successful founders aren't jerks, so they don't get the same attention. It's a mistake to conflate aggression and abrasiveness with strength and decisiveness.

Fourth, the true drivers of a founder's success are often less visible and more nuanced. Qualities like resilience, strategic thinking, and building and leading strong teams are critical. These are not the traits of a jerk but of a reflective and adaptable leader. The truth is that success is multifaceted.

Jobs, for example, was not just an asshole; he was also a master strategist with an uncanny ability to anticipate market trends and consumer desires. Musk showed immense resilience during the early years of SpaceX and Tesla, which were both considered crazy bets at the time. Ellison helped pioneer the relational database model when he founded Oracle in 1977 and pursued a relentless acquisition strategy afterward to keep his company viable. Bezos studiously plowed every cent of his free cash flow back into Amazon for over two decades before finally deciding his business was durable enough to start turning a profit.

Jobs was not successful because he was a jerk; he was successful because *he changed*. He learned how to spot talent, to encourage cooperation, to recognize the importance of systems. Ultimately, he tamed his toxic narcissism. Adam Neumann never did, and it all blew up (well, sort of—he was later funded by Andreessen Horowitz, who stated they like "seeing repeat-founders build on past successes by growing from lessons learned").[5]

How do we know this to be true? It turns out the evidence is right there in Rich's 30 years of research.

Dispelling the Myth with Data

A few years ago, Rich realized he had amassed enough data to start answering the big question: What are the core differences between successful and unsuccessful founders? Rich began to coach founders in 2009, and over the last 15 years, he has built a database of 360-degree ratings for each of the 46 competencies for every founder he has coached. Each of these 46 competencies has proven over the decades to be highly correlated with effective leadership, not just for founders but for anyone in a leadership position.

After checking for data quality and completeness, Rich began to conduct an exploratory data analysis. For example, what designates a "successful founder"? As mentioned earlier in the methodology, using MOIC (multiple on invested capital), a measure of return on investment, the founders who generated 10x returns were selected as the standard for success. They represented the top 21% of all founders. Then Rich identified the most significant leadership competencies that influenced their success by running a stepwise discriminant analysis, as well as various other statistical modeling techniques. He then conducted validation modeling to check the results.

And after several years of rigorous statistical analysis, patterns began to emerge.

The 15 Key Leadership Competencies That Differentiate Successful and Unsuccessful Founders

Out of the 46 leadership competencies that Rich tracked, 15 were found to be statistically significant between the successful founder cohort and the unsuccessful one. Using factor analysis, Rich found that these competencies tended to show up in four different clusters, meaning if a founder demonstrated strength (or weakness) in one of the competencies, they tended to demonstrate the same ratings for the rest of the cluster.

All of a sudden, the answers became clear:

- Successful founders are **adaptable**.
- Successful founders **work through others**.
- Successful founders **understand the importance of scaling**.
- Successful founders have strong **personal grounding**.

We are also including a chapter on **self-awareness**, a crucial proficiency that spans across all of the four key differentiating clusters mentioned above. When we dig deeper into the data looking for broader themes, we find that self-awareness is the "phantom planet" that exerts its gravity across this entire constellation of competencies.

Real Talk from Stakeholders: Bringing the Data to Life

As we mentioned in the methodology, along with ratings of leadership competencies and personality profiles for each founder, Rich had thousands of comments from people who worked with these leaders, which helped bring all this data to life.

From the nearly 5,000 pages of 360 feedback comments, themes and patterns were analyzed for all founders, both successful and unsuccessful. This was done to identify broad patterns and to compare founders on individual skills. AI tools were used to find themes in a treasure trove of comments.

This section of the book explores the true differences between successful and unsuccessful founders. Again, this all comes from the data. The pattern linking all of these independent competencies to financial success has surfaced through rigorous statistical analysis. This isn't an exercise in cherry-picking or flower arranging.

Let's start with our first cluster of differentiating competencies: adaptability.

CHAPTER 4

Adaptability: Because Product-Market Fit Is Never Done

M eet your typical college dropout founder. He doesn't go to classes. He doesn't go to parties. Instead, he's obsessed with his vision for an "everything app" that can do it all: messaging, payments, transportation, e-commerce, entertainment. With the help of an angel investor, he moves out of his Ivy League dorm to the peninsula and begins building his product and his team.

The first year is great: The app has plenty of buzz, the team grows to 30 people, and more investment money piles in. He feels on top of the world. But the cracks are already starting to show. He has always been obsessive, but now he has trouble letting go of small things: pet features, lost arguments, perceived slights. He fixates on everything that deviates from his original vision. *But that's what all founders are like*, he figures.

Suddenly, several new copycat competitors show up on the app charts. His product manager shows him some product ideas to stay ahead of the curve, but he dismisses all of them as derivative. As the company gets bigger, the board asks him to hire more experienced executives. But he dismisses their "big company culture," and great candidates then tell the board that they have no interest in working with him. The board, in turn, reaches out to Rich.

The founder tells Rich that his team seems to be actively conspiring against him. He knows his original idea is still solid, but suddenly, everyone is a critic. If his people aren't going to work with him, he is just going to have to work without them.

Rich reminds him that in startups, the only constant is change. He needs to be wary of inflexibility. What got him to this stage won't get him to the next one. He needs to do a better job of working with his team in order to (a) adapt to new circumstances and (b) create buy-in. He needs to stay nimble. He's in a different environment now, so he needs to adapt.

But didn't people "buy into" his idea when they decided to work for his company in the first place? And besides, don't you *have* to be ridiculously stubborn to get a successful product into the market? Isn't that part of the job description?

The founder turns inward. He assumes that if he shares anything, it's eventually going to be used against him, so he closes down. When he's not lashing out at someone, he's sulking in his corner office. He can't understand why people don't just stick to the strategy.

Growth begins to stall. His CFO tells him they have six months left. They have to make a move. Find a new direction. Lots of great companies made early strategic pivots. But what's the point of pivoting when you still haven't landed your original idea? *Everyone just needs to do their job*, he thinks. *Stick to the plan. It'll work out.*

It doesn't work out.

The Adaptability Cluster

When we look through our 15 differentiating competencies between successful and unsuccessful founders, we see a clearly related cluster:

- Openness to input
- Handling resistance to change
- Creating buy-in

In other words, successful founders tend to do all three of these things better. But not only that—if they do *one* of these things better, they tend to do *all of them* better.

From a distance, this competency cluster deals with the ability to listen to new ideas, handle criticism, react to the market, make smart adjustments, and rally people in your new direction. But what's really going on here? What's the unifying theme behind all these activities?

Adaptability.

What makes adaptability such a fundamental part of founder success? And why do so many founders struggle with it? After all, aren't *most* founders squirrel-brained whiz kids with a penchant for pivots? So, what trips them up when it comes to effective adaptability? And what can they do about it?

At first, we were puzzled by the presence of this cluster as a differentiator between successful and unsuccessful founders. After all, when we look at all 122 founders in our dataset, they average well above the mean on adaptability. As a group, it's a strength. This shouldn't be an issue.

But then we dug a little deeper and made a surprising discovery. As it turns out, while *most* founders are adaptable, unsuccessful founders are decidedly *not*. Their numbers are deep in the red on this competency. In fact, they significantly drag down the mean. The data is loud and clear—a *lack* of adaptability, or rigidity, is a massive Achilles' heel for unsuccessful founders.

So we decided to explore further. As we dug further into the data, we were able (in a Hubble Space Telescope–like way) to get a much more detailed picture of this multifaceted competency. And some of those facets might strike you as odd and surprising.

Product-Market Fit Is Never Done

Why is adaptability so important for founders? It's very simple: To effectively develop the rest of the competencies in this book, it will help tremendously *if you're still in business*. Without adaptability, that's a very unlikely prospect.

Many in the industry like to talk about product-market fit—or the stage at which a product meets the needs of a market in a way that creates significant demand and growth—as if it's a static event, a ribbon at the end of a race. But in practice, there is no finish line: markets evolve, competitors rise, customer expectations mature, technology advances. In response to this universal truth, adaptable founders have developed an iterative mindset fueled by ferocious intellectual curiosity, a confident tolerance for ambiguity, and a bias toward action.

All founders love their original idea. After all, it was the spark that launched the entire enterprise: the funding, the talent, the execution, the product. But if things go well, that also means that things get complicated. Suddenly, you're dealing with lots of smart people with sharp opinions. There are multiple strategic paths to consider. There are biases to negotiate, arguments to engage, threats to weigh. You may have closed an initial cohort of customers with your vision, but which are truly good fits and which are empty calories?

Maybe you were able to land an early product fit back when your company was a small team bossed around by a benign dictator who had their hand in everything (or maybe you just got lucky). But to keep hitting that floating target you will need to stay (a) disciplined and (b) flexible. That might sound contradictory, but it's what makes adaptability such a fascinating competency to explore.

Rich defines "adaptability" as the ability to "adjust rapidly to changing situations and priorities, tolerate ambiguity, and develop new ways of behaving in order to achieve objectives and get around obstacles." Adaptable founders are the sails of the ship. They capture and direct market momentum. They keep adjusting to new developments, information, opportunities, and problems. They are perpetually open-minded and curious. They encourage an experimental "Let's give it a shot and see how it works" approach that can propel the entire organization: "He does a great job of crossing disciplines, studying up, and becoming effective in new areas."

When we dig deeper into the internal personality data and the external 360 comments of adaptable founders, we find that these iterative leaders share several common traits.

They appear *comfortable with uncertainty*. They thrive on ambiguity and use it to their advantage. They enjoy the challenge of navigating unclear situations: "Handles ambiguity better than I do and is always finding a novel approach to a difficult problem." They understand that they'll never have all the information and see themselves as an ongoing project: "He is a learning machine. He continues to grow and evolve." As a result, their behavior becomes infectious: "Thrives on rapid change and encourages it."

They are incredibly *responsive*. They adjust quickly to changing situations and priorities. They are quick decision-makers and can pivot strategies effectively. They are constantly iterating: "One of his great strengths is thinking originally and divorcing himself from legacy mindsets very quickly." As a result, they inspire others to welcome change as an opportunity for growth: "She isn't afraid of change and disruption, and it's been critical to our growth and survival."

They are also notably adept at *context shifting*. As Tien says, "On any given day I might have to attend a board meeting, take a customer call, coach an executive, talk to an investor, go to a quarterly sales meeting, prep for an all-hands—the list goes on. In each one of those meetings, I have to be somebody different."

These founders are Swiss Army Knives. They constantly impress their coworkers with their ability to adapt to any situation: "Very adaptable and agile to suit the requirements of the constantly evolving industry."

Adaptability is the engine that powers the following three competencies.

Openness to Input

These founders solicit and are open to feedback and differing ideas and views. They avoid intimidation or domination, and welcome suggestions.
—Rich Hagberg

As Stephen Covey notes: "Most people don't listen with the intent to understand; they listen with the intent to reply."[1] The best founders maintain a beginner's mind rooted in keeping focus, valuing the messenger, and sustaining curiosity.

"Marc Benioff would talk about the beginner's mind all the time," says Tien. "It takes work to approach a new challenge with a lack of preconceptions. To approach it with humility and curiosity, with fresh eyes and an open mind."

As Matt Blumberg notes in *Startup CEO*: "Just being present and not multitasking in meetings as a leader is important but it isn't enough. It's always better to ask questions, listen to conversations, and shape them around the edges—rather than shutting down the conversation by diving in with the answer at the onset of a debate."[2]

The problem is that in the early stages, founders *actually do know more* about the organization than anyone else. But at a certain point, they inevitably lose touch with certain aspects of the business. The adaptable ones, however, welcome this development. They appreciate that they've reached a certain stage where they can bring in seasoned perspectives, giving them more information to make better decisions.

A thematic analysis of their 360 reviews shows that they are also deeply motivated by *personal growth and development*. They look at feedback as an opportunity for improvement. They are genuinely interested in what people say because they're curious and want to expand their sphere of knowledge in a disciplined way: "She is constantly trying to adapt as a leader to get around obstacles."

Handling Resistance to Change

These founders identify sources of resistance to change and effectively deal with them before they undermine change initiatives.
—Rich Hagberg

We all have heard stories of pivots that seemed brilliant in hindsight. Slack started as an in-house messaging system for a failed electronic game. Twitter (X) started as a podcast platform. Android started as an operating system for cameras. Instagram started as a Foursquare-type app called Burbn. Pay-Pal started as a way to exchange money between PalmPilots. Pinterest used to be a mobile shopping app called Tote. Rovio made 50 games before they found success with *Angry Birds*.

But as we know, hindsight is 20/20. The reality is that pivots are excruciating experiences. Change can feel threatening to employees. It inevitably challenges status, influence, self-worth, or a general desire for stability and "the way things used to work." As companies mature, the old-timers who miss the early freewheeling days might resent the new structure. And so the antibodies will attack.

Adaptable founders handle this resistance by being *empathetic*—listening to the input of those who resist, and genuinely understanding their concerns (after all, they might discover something they otherwise would have missed). These founders self-report that they try to talk about things they need from people in terms of their direct reports' own desires and preferences.

They balance their innate assertiveness with a broader sensitivity to the team's concerns: "She has a sixth sense when it comes to company morale and identifies potential areas of concern before pushing new ideas or initiatives." And they know how to find their inner Oprah: "He has a gift for sensing people's emotional states. He can effectively move people to a place of acceptance."

However, once they decide to present their plan of action, they are incredibly *persuasive*. They are socially adroit—they state that sometimes by agreeing with someone, they can gradually get that person around to their way of thinking. They create a "burning platform" that helps people understand the dire threat of stasis and the rationale for pursuing a new direction.

They are *diplomatic*—they know how to speak differently to different audiences: "She told us that we had a big problem coming with new competitors and that we needed to change our go-to-market, but she had a plan to address it. There were going to be obstacles, but we could overcome them together. We had to act decisively but not impulsively. And she was right."

They might even "create" a precipitating event to speed that change along. Right before Salesforce launched, the engineering team was clamoring for more time for QA and bug fixes. But then Marc Benioff calmly mentioned that he had just told the *Wall Street Journal* that they would be launching in a couple of days: "So what do you guys want to do?" The site launched, and everything went fine. It was the right move. Benioff knew they were ready, so he created a nice little forcing function.

Creating Buy-In

These founders excel at building commitment and winning support for initiatives through personal and professional credibility, trustworthiness, persuasive communication, stakeholder involvement, and aligning expectations.
—Rich Hagberg

Adaptable founders recognize a simple truth: the capacity for an organization to change will always be *far less* than the capacity for a founder to think up new reasons to change. They understand that when people feel that their idea has been given a fair hearing, they are less likely to resist, even if they ultimately don't get what they want.

Take the strategic planning process. A canny founder will think to themselves: *Even though I think I know the direction we need to pursue, I'll let the team get there on their own.* Why? Because the founder knows that when the team builds the strategy—when everyone feels heard, and the rationale is clear and transparent—they will *own* that strategy. They won't be simply responding to orders.

These founders *trust their team.* Successful founders are much more likely to agree with a statement that says that most of their coworkers can be trusted to work hard, even when the boss is not around (their opposites strongly disagree). They genuinely believe in their people, which gives them the time and space to anticipate challenges and adjust accordingly.

They recognize the value of leveraging their team's strengths, so they present them with challenges they're excited about (engineers, for example, react to interesting problems, not dictated solutions). This process turns employees into partners: "He does a great job of building consensus by identifying and involving all the key stakeholders. I feel like I'm a valued part of the process."

They also create buy-in by *modeling the way forward*: "Everyone knows he bleeds for this company, so we take what he says very seriously when it comes to new projects." They're confident—they self-report that they genuinely enjoy sharing their opinions in front of a group. They are also genuinely positive—they note that they seem to worry about things less than other people do.

Their ability to negotiate win-win solutions prevents conflicts from escalating: "He always wins support for new initiatives because he is so honestly transparent as well as relentlessly positive." They understand the need to be receptive and accessible: "Quick on his feet to respond to shifting priorities—one of his strongest points."

There's also a very cold, mercenary argument for listening to people: you might learn something new.

Why Founders Struggle with Adaptability

As we discussed earlier, founders tend to be a pretty adaptable bunch (and that's not just survivorship bias talking—we have the data). They have to navigate treacherous waters, switch strategies, and continuously innovate.

So why, even within this inherently flexible group of humans, do so many of them struggle with adaptability? This is where Rich's personality data really gives us the insights. When we combine founders' personality assessments (their own opinions of their needs, behavioral tendencies, emotional reactions, cognitive approach, social style, and general identity) with their behavioral 360 ratings, some clear patterns begin to emerge.

It's an ironic truth—founders, who are notoriously averse to bureaucracy and organizational inertia, *tend to generate lots of it*. They either pontificate and prevaricate, or they jump wildly at every opportunity, immolating their team members in the process. They don't allow themselves to be open to different experiences and perspectives, so they become the obstacle instead of the accelerant. They slow everything down.

These founders might appear adaptable (chasing after the latest trends, obsessing over the competition, etc.), but their personality scores reveal that they're actually incredibly *rigid*. They talk the talk, but they don't walk the walk. They struggle to let go. They prefer to stick to familiar methods that have worked in the past. They tend to anchor around past successes.

In short, their general cognitive posture is *closed*, not open: "Does not appear that he has developed as a leader. Instead, he tends to avoid leading by locking himself in the back room." They consider themselves completed projects, so they can't be bothered to ask for advice: "He seems completely unable to change his behavior. He keeps approaching problems the same way, hoping for a different result."

They admit they *hate ambiguity*, so they perceive change as a threat. They much prefer clearly defined situations. They desperately seek black-and-white answers in a world of shades of gray: "Has very little tolerance for ambiguity—most discussions and worldviews are presented as black and white without nuance." As a result, they struggle to make decisions based on incomplete information (i.e., practically every single one): "He has a real problem with analysis paralysis."

They're exceptionally *mistrustful*. They're much more likely to believe overly optimistic people have a naive view of the world. They also describe themselves as being incredibly selective about who they choose to open up to. Here's another jaw-dropper: "He defers communication, and you often learn about things through an accidental path. You might be uninvited to a meeting or become aware of a new reporting structure by reading it in a new presentation. At the end of the day, we are all people and want to be treated like we matter. The least you could do is look us in the eye when you deliver your decisions."

These founders are seen as profoundly *dictatorial*—when you don't listen, it's difficult to recognize the need to change. They self-report that people find it very hard to convince them that they are wrong on a point(!). To the surprise of no one but themselves, there's a marked difference between their own perceived capabilities in their self-reported personality tests and the frank assessments of their coworkers: "He needs to feel like you know exactly what you are doing, and he does not adjust his behavior. He is who he is, and gets passionate and loud, thinking that it is going to yield the result he wants."

So they come across as headstrong assholes, pushing for their own views, resisting disagreement, and generally ruining everyone's lives: "He assumes the original model will work, or that the new model recommended to him was what he was thinking all along. He does not seem to be able to keep all interdependencies in mind when recommending solutions." They are momentum killers: "He creates the ambiguity and then becomes the obstacle. He gets very upset and negative when he doesn't get his way or gets pushback on a project."

Their self-reported personality scores also reveal that they are profoundly *anxious*, *insecure*, and *secretive*. They tend to see other people as antagonists, so they hold their decisions tight to their chests. Instead of seeking change and opportunity, they build walls and silos: "I often worry that he has Machiavellian tendencies when it comes to getting things done. He has explicitly told me not to tell people what I'm really doing or tell them something else instead of what is actually happening."

The result is a vicious circle. They are aware their job performance is negatively impacted by their behavior and admit to getting upset when criticized, *but that only reinforces their rigid approach.* They suffer from high anxiety, pessimism about the future, and low energy levels, but they have zero ability to recognize that *they* are the cause of all this consternation. Unsurprisingly, their 360 comments show that they plainly suck at team building and inspiring people. They often share this awareness, but the tragedy is that their response is to circle the wagons.

They also *struggle to empower and delegate*, so they can't enable change: "He doesn't have to get better at working on the product himself. He just has to learn to empower the great team he put together." As a result, their stakeholders feel unheard and undervalued, resulting in a quiet reluctance to support decisions made in such a blatantly dictatorial manner: "He defaults to telling you your commitments, as opposed to leading you there."

Their *impatience* and *instability* prevent them from thoughtfully considering feedback or adapting their strategies, contributing to their lack of adaptability. They score low on patience and high on time urgency. They strongly agree with a statement that says they get frustrated by people who can't make quick decisions.

As a result, they are perpetually *stressed*. They're completely strung out. They confess that they find it difficult to concentrate, and sometimes they don't even have the energy to think. They also self-report that their job performance is affected because they are frequently upset. So they make more impulsive decisions, they make more dictatorial statements, and the doom loop rolls on.

So, what concrete steps can you take to increase your adaptability?

Moving Forward

If you're struggling with adaptability, your ego is probably clouding your ability to listen, respond, and bring people along.

Stop playing the tyrant. Be aware of your own warping effect when it comes to group dynamics. Here's a suggestion from Tien: Head into your next meeting telling yourself that you're *only allowed to ask questions*, not make declarative statements of any kind. This will feel like pulling teeth at first, but it will open up new insights.

Develop a relationship with ambiguity. Many things are beyond your control. Focus on what is tangible and achievable—and don't worry about the rest. Look at unseen challenges and curveballs as opportunities to learn something new. Want a Benioff-approved reading suggestion? *Zen Mind, Beginner's Mind* by Shunryu Suzuki.[3]

Stop spreading yourself thin. Address your inability to let go of things. Your job is simply to find the biggest problem (there's always one), fix it, then move on to the next one—that's it. Prioritize. Pick your battles, and delegate everything else. Protect your focus and avoid the death of a thousand cuts.

Interrogate your decision-making. Encourage other people to question your assumptions and push you to consider what might go wrong: "What am I missing? Why might my approach fail?" Consider yourself a perpetual learning project. Make a habit of reading, taking courses, or attending workshops that push you out of your comfort zone and help you develop new perspectives.

Trust your people. Give them challenges. Start with small tasks and gradually increase the level of delegation. Provide support and guidance when needed, but allow them to come up with their own solutions.

Be proactive about addressing your stress. Find out what works for you: meditation, exercise, a hobby that preferably has nothing to do with technology. Learn how to take a break. Tien likes to take a couple of weeks off every year in order to "let the company run itself."

Ask yourself: Is there anything else going on internally that's affecting your ability to iterate? Is your relationship suffering because of work? Any unresolved grief or trauma issues? It might be time to think about consulting a shrink. Walking through that door for the first time will be painful, but it's invariably worth the effort.

Ultimately, the data doesn't lie: Adaptability isn't just a competency that's "nice to have." It's an imperative. It's not only a pathway to personal growth but a key driver of business success.

This brings us to the next step in the never-ending quest to find product-market fit: working through others.

CHAPTER 5

Working Through Others: From Loners to Leaders

This person is the dictionary definition of "founder mode." A brilliant developer and a visionary thinker, he quickly attracts initial investment and a team of top-tier talent. At the outset, his team thrives on his energy and ideas. His technical skills are unparalleled, and his passion for innovation is contagious. He works tirelessly, coding through nights and orchestrating every aspect of the company, from product development to marketing. He reviews every line of code, dictates marketing strategies, and scrutinizes minor operational decisions.

As the team expands, however, his insistence on controlling everything creates bottlenecks. Brilliant engineers and creative marketers spend more time waiting for his approval than putting their ideas into practice. Meetings become hectoring lectures—he only transmits; he does not receive. His general MO is to hold people to incredibly high standards and then let them sink or swim.

Developing the flagship product is a particularly nightmarish experience. The founder's meticulous attention to detail, which had initially been an asset, now becomes a potentially fatal liability. He constantly changes specifications, refuses to delegate crucial tasks, and ignores the advice of his experienced engineers. The development process drags on longer than expected, causing frustration and burnout among the team.

His charisma continues to attract investors, but the internal fissures are growing wider. Morale plummets, and the once collaborative culture deteriorates into one of fear and competition. The careerists are more focused on appeasing the founder than on driving the company forward. If his company has had a culture at all, it's inspired by "The Emperor's New Clothes." A board member reaches out to Rich.

When Rich presents the founder with his inevitably dismal 360 ratings, the founder dismisses them out of hand. "They don't get it," he says. "They don't see the whole picture like I do. I'm smarter than most of them, and I'm the one who knows what's best for this company." He genuinely believes he is always right and that his intelligence places him above the perspectives of those around him. He often says things like, "If I listened to them, we'd be going in circles. I see what they don't."

Rich tells him: "You've hired talented people. They have functional expertise that you simply don't have. Trust them to do their jobs. You can't grow a company if you're managing every detail yourself. I know you don't believe this, but you have become the biggest obstacle."

The departure of a key hire from a leading AI company sends shockwaves through the team. It becomes a tipping point, leading other engineers to reconsider their positions. The slow, agonizing exodus of talent begins, leaving the company struggling to maintain its momentum. Employees warn their friends away. Nasty reviews start showing up on Glassdoor.

With the team in disarray, the product launch is delayed. Investors grow anxious, sensing the underlying turmoil. Despite the mounting pressure (or perhaps because of it), the founder continues to go it alone, firing off unilateral decisions over Slack without consulting what is left of his leadership team.

The product finally launches not with a bang, but a whimper. Bugs that could have been caught with proper team input and testing mar the release. The complaints flood in. The team gets slammed. They turn inward. Competitors pounce, pushing the company further behind in the market.

Eventually, the founder tries to make amends and cut people some slack, but it's too little too late. He never really built any genuine relationships, so there's very little material to mend in the first place. The company limps along into mediocrity, becoming what Maynard Webb calls a "tweener"—neither a breakout hit nor a complete failure.

A tragedy. Rich still thinks about him sometimes. If he had just been willing to grow—if he had taken the feedback seriously, trusted his team, and learned to manage his emotions—his company could have been a massive success. Leadership isn't just about having the right vision; it's about empowering the people around you to help bring that vision to life. And unfortunately, that's a lesson this founder never learned.

Your People Are Your Leverage

Archimedes had a famous line about the power of the lever: "Give me a place to stand, and I shall move the earth." But what constitutes a lever in a startup? These days, it's less about capital mechanics or raw materials and more about human intellect. People are your leverage. Work through them, and you shall move the earth.

But here's the dirty little secret: Most founders don't care what other people think. That's not really in their nature. Not caring about what people think is what got them the job in the first place! Founders generally don't get funding for their people skills. They are usually given the green light for the potential of their idea and the foundations of their personality: ferocious nonconformity, comfort with ambiguity, aggressiveness, competitiveness. All of which can be absolutely corrosive to building cohesive teams. Founders, to risk another metaphor, are poison pills.

In his book *David and Goliath*, Malcolm Gladwell tells the story of Dr. Emil "Jay" Freireich, who single-handedly turned childhood leukemia into a treatable disease by employing all kinds of provocative and aggressive new techniques that set his colleagues' collective hair on fire.[1] This attitude works up to a point (it's obviously much easier when you're an individual researcher). It's difficult to motivate and organize a group of people when you essentially hold their opinions in disdain. Even though most founders share the Freireich line of thinking, the successful ones have avoided the time bomb trap by effectively leveraging the talents and perspectives of others.

When we look through the data, we find a second cluster that is strongly correlated (meaning these traits tend to show up either as a group or not at all). Successful founders tend to score above the mean on all the following:

- Building teams
- Delegation and empowerment
- Relationship building

The picture that emerges from this group of skills is clear: Successful founders learn how to work effectively with other people, and unsuccessful founders do not.

That seems like a fairly straightforward point, but there's a cruel paradox sitting at the heart of this chapter. The "Working Through Others" cluster, which is essential to success, *sits in direct opposition to the fundamental attributes of founders*. It's simply not who they are. But you need both halves to succeed. You need to be a forceful leader *and* an empathetic organizer, a wide-eyed visionary *and* a detail-oriented driver of discipline, a ruthless competitor *and* a supportive mentor.

For most founders, finding proficiency within these competencies constitutes a trial by fire—the fire, in this case, being the presence of other human beings with ideas and convictions of their own. But plenty of founders have managed to make the leap from loner to leader.

Building Teams

These founders model and encourage teamwork by
fostering cooperation, communication, trust, shared goals,
interdependency, and mutual accountability and support.
—Rich Hagberg

To many founders, team building is alien territory, terra incognita. It's like the difference between theory and practice—or knowing of the presence of a foreign country versus actually visiting it. Many of Rich's clients realize the importance of teams, but they have very little practical experience in building them.

Most founders are natural loners. They didn't play sports in high school. They weren't on the team. Lots of them were playing video games, or coding, or smoking pot, or executing some combination of the three. They've never experienced real teamwork, so they don't really understand it. They do not trust that others are as smart, clever, or creative as they are. They want to turn their vision into reality, but they want firm control of that process. They might give lip service to the value of organized effort, but they're actually deeply mistrustful of the basic concept.

That's understandable. It's hard to truly believe in something you've never truly experienced. What does it feel like to be on a team that's really humming, working smoothly together, and hitting its numbers? What does it feel like to be on a team that's been knocked down but survives and succeeds in the face of big challenges? What does this concept of synergy actually look and feel like? Lots of founders have no idea.

So they manage their teams in a "hub and spoke" style, preferring one-on-one conversations over collaborative meetings, and they wind up creating silos and misinformation. Or they make unilateral decisions, leaving their team members feeling isolated and unheard. Or they push conflicts under the rug, where those issues proceed to grow and metastasize. Ultimately, it's the team who suffers. They can't create. They can't execute. They can't reach their full potential.

So, is this a hopeless pursuit? Not at all. Team building is a *craft*. It's a skill that can be learned. No one is born with it. Maybe you missed out on it in high school, but that doesn't mean you can't learn the fundamentals. A lot of founders, being nerds at heart, start off by reading books: *The Five Dysfunctions of a Team, Leaders Eat Last, The Culture Code*.[2] They develop internal frameworks. They ask for advice from investors and board members. They start paying more attention to their personal dynamics and others around them. That's all fine and well.

But eventually, the successful ones realize that they need to completely redefine their jobs. Their new full-time gig is building teams.

Because if they don't, they're missing out on the insights of others. That puts them at a huge strategic disadvantage. Lots of corporate executives are very good at this stuff because they've received the training and taken it seriously. For founders, it's another story. The inability to bring people together is another perennial Achilles' heel. Success in the startup space hinges on collective effort, and our data underscores the need for a balance between independence and interdependence, between demanding excellence and nurturing capability.

So what happens when we look at the differentiating personality traits of founders who are good at building teams versus those who struggle with this competency? We find . . . nothing. Well, not nothing. We find a few crumbs. But that's good news! It means that learning how to build teams is a *skill*. It's not an intrinsic gift.

Our research suggests that founders who build strong teams simply do a better job of *listening to people*. Or at least they appear to, anyway. Their colleagues agree: "He is very loyal to his team, and very approachable. Even when I disagree with his decisions, I feel like he gives me a fair hearing." Being founders, they may not actually care what someone thinks of a particular topic, but they know that it's important *to make them feel like they do*. So yes, sometimes, they go through the motions. But everyone walks away satisfied.

Externally, they win praise for building a sense of *shared identity and fate*. They do this by facilitating collective answers to the fundamental questions: Why does the team exist? What should it be trying to accomplish? Where can we add value? How should it best focus its time and resources to help the organization succeed? They include people in the creation of the strategy. They create collective buy-in rather than simply mandating results: "Every deal we have or are currently working on is a group effort; he keeps us all involved in the momentum."

In general, they are much more *socially adroit*. They self-report that they talk about things they might need from people in terms of their audience's own desires and preferences. They are also happy to concede that in most situations, they usually agree with the opinions of the group. They're not conformers—these people are still very headstrong. Relative to their unsuccessful peers, however, they are simply *much more cognizant* of the concerns and opinions of others and of the importance of speaking to them in a language they understand.

What's the difference between an empathetic organizer and a canny manipulator? When it comes to founders, perhaps not much. But the successful ones seem to be much better at listening, thinking, and responding in terms of someone else's perspective. And as a result, they are much more effective at binding collective effort.

Delegation and Empowerment

These founders place trust in others by moving decision-making closer to the level where the work is done and by giving others the responsibility, authority, independence, and support they need to succeed.
—Rich Hagberg

At some point, every founder needs to shift from being a soloist to being a conductor. You need to start prioritizing collective harmony over individual notes. You have to let go of perfectionism and accept that others might do things differently but still get results. For founders, this is pure torture. This painful dynamic is captured in this exchange between a founder and a business executive in the great 2023 film *BlackBerry*:

Mike: So, there's a reason why your intercom is emitting white noise. It's because it was manufactured by engineers who didn't care, and now every office in the world has to suffer an annoying hiss, a blinking red light, 15 different power cords that are utterly incompatible with one another. So, uh. We are not doing that. We are not just adding to the hiss. I will build a prototype, but I'll do it perfectly or I don't do it.

Jim: Mike, are you familiar with the saying "Perfect is the enemy of good"?
Mike: Well, "good enough" is the enemy of humanity.

As much as it pains you, you need to trust other people to figure things out their own way. You should accept that certain processes might move slower before they get faster. This is not a simple process. First, you need to assess whether an individual has demonstrated good judgment and the ability to achieve results when given independence. Next, you need to balance oversight and autonomy—monitoring progress without micromanaging, and providing just enough guidance to ensure tasks are on track while giving people the room to innovate. Delegation doesn't mean throwing someone in the deep end. You need to provide ongoing feedback and support.

But all founders eventually have to make the leap. They have to reset their thinking and reconceptualize their roles. They have to transition from a jack-of-all-trades to a team builder—because if you don't learn how to delegate tasks and responsibilities, you will ultimately become a roadblock and will burn yourself out. You cannot and should not try to do everything or be involved in every meeting.

The founders who rank high on delegation excel at setting *clear expectations*. They lucidly communicate what success looks like, what needs to be done, and who is responsible. They empower their team by gradually transitioning from task delegation to granting broad responsibilities and ownership of initiatives: "I wake up every morning knowing the task at hand, and the reasons for doing it. I credit that to our CEO, who obviously makes an effort to ensure that everyone is on the same page."

They are more *patient in bringing people along*. They're described as generally pretty chill. They self-report that they don't become annoyed if the driver in front of them dawdles a little after the stoplight turns green. They give people the space they need to execute: "She's not a micromanager. She empowers others to address challenges or goals with a minimum of interference." They understand that success takes time. They know they probably won't be satisfied with someone's first try. But with every turn of the wheel, they'll get closer to the promised land: "He sets up key metrics, then gives teams lots of discretion in how to hit those metrics."

They're *stable*, which gives their team members the confidence to try new things and not worry about getting chewed out if something goes wrong. They understand that startling ideas often come from stable environments. They recognize that mistrust and negativity are corrosive to creativity. Their employees feel comfortable taking risks and seizing initiatives because they feel supported: "I feel comfortable trying new approaches because I know he has my back."

Ultimately, however, they *hold people accountable*. They understand that the ultimate goal is results. They're composed (they note that they're fine repeating things until they're understood), but they're firm. They're much more willing to give direct feedback rather than let frustrations linger: "What you see is what you get, and he has no issue at all communicating very direct feedback at all times. If things aren't working well, he'll let you know, but he'll also work with you to find a way forward."

Rethinking Founder Mode

Delegation certainly has its challenges. If you're not careful, it can devolve into benign neglect, leaving you clueless about the actual state of your company. As the investor Paul Graham notes in his now-famous post on "Founder Mode":

> Hire good people and give them room to do their jobs. Sounds great when it's described that way, doesn't it? Except in practice, judging from the report of founder after founder, what this often turns out to mean is: hire professional fakers and let them drive the company into the ground.[3]

This is a fair point. In many ways, today's standard corporate structure seems almost *designed* to gaslight founders. It's a huge struggle to resist mental biases and maintain organizational awareness when you're surrounded by intelligent careerists who are incentivized to only share good news (otherwise known as "managing up").

So what's the alternative? What exactly is "founder mode"? Graham, a canny observer of external trends, doesn't presume to know the entire answer, but he suggests that periodically escaping the C-suite is certainly part of it:

> Whatever founder mode consists of, it's pretty clear that it's going to break the principle that the CEO should engage with the company only via his or her direct reports. 'Skip-level' meetings will become the norm instead of a practice so unusual that there's a name for it. And once you abandon that constraint there are a huge number of permutations to choose from.

Airbnb founder Brian Chesky furthers the idea in a podcast: "The less hands-on I was, the more I got sucked into problems. And by the time I got sucked into a problem, it was like 10 times as much work." Instead, he decides: "I'm going to be involved in every single detail. And Airbnb is not going to do anything more than I can personally focus on."[4]

On the surface, this sounds like good advice. After all, founders have a unique institutional expertise. They know where all the bodies are buried. They should be the ones fixing the big problems. Also, crucially, *founders are not managers*. It doesn't make sense for them to pretend otherwise. Some notable founder mode examples include people like Mark Zuckerberg, Sam Altman, Elon Musk, Jensen Huang, and Steve Jobs.

But what if this hands-on approach is precisely why many startups stumble? While founder mode has a certain contrarian appeal, it glosses over a critical truth: Most founders who refuse to step out of their early hyper-involved roles struggle to scale their companies effectively. Many burn out, lose focus, and create bottlenecks. Our research indicates that clinging too tightly to founder mode can hinder, not help, long-term success.

Here's our take on founder mode: Delegation is a superpower, not a weakness. It's not about abandoning your vision, it's about empowering others to carry it forward. Delegation is not a sign of disinterest but a strategic move to ensure the company can grow without being limited by one person. Founders who continue to treat their companies as if they're still a team of 20 employees will fail to adapt to the demands of a growing business. They'll fail the time bomb test.

Crucially, the most successful founders don't remain locked into founder mode indefinitely—*they evolve.* They understand that while their initial involvement was critical to getting the company off the ground, long-term success requires a shift in leadership style, strategic delegation, and empowering others to lead. Here some notable examples include Satya Nadella and Tim Cook.

Effective delegators are the opposite of checked-out and clueless. They are nimble innovators who develop their leadership style as their company grows, moving fluidly between hands-on involvement and strategic delegation. As a result, they can evolve, empower, and scale.

Relationship Building

> *Founders who excel at relationship building are friendly, open, and approachable. They cultivate trusting relationships that are maintained over time.*
> —Rich Hagberg

Startup teams operate within a unique kind of hell. Most of the time, they operate with limited resources: budget, head count, time. They are expected to be canny and resourceful, stretching what they have to cover a huge range of activities. Stress, long hours, blurred roles, harsh pivots—this is all a recipe for burnout or crippled performance if not managed carefully.

They have to move fast. The decision-making process in startups is quicker and more fluid than in, say, a bank. Teams need to make decisions swiftly, often with incomplete information. There's often a mismatch between goals and abilities. Maintaining cohesion and culture during scaling is hard. Balancing speed with due diligence is a tightrope act. There's a huge pressure to emphasize results over relationships.

Startup teams are also much more emotionally invested than in typical corporate environments. In general, that's a positive thing, but personal investment and bruised egos tend to go hand in hand. Everyone knows which buttons to push. When individual agendas get in the way, things can quickly run off the rails.

The founders who rate high on relationship building display a *genuine interest in others*. They take the time to ask about personal interests, family, and aspirations. They're okay with small talk. They're curious about people in addition to ideas. They are happy to admit that they enjoy working with people of various beliefs and cultural backgrounds.

As a result, their colleagues feel truly heard. Of course, they're also cognizant of the fact that personal engagement fosters a more supportive, creative work environment: "He takes the time to ask about my family, my interests, what's going on in my life. He's really good at that stuff."

They are *approachable* and *inclusive*. They have the self-awareness to understand how their position of authority tends to warp the dynamic with their employees. So they set an amenable tone. They self-report that they feel a deep obligation to meet their commitments to their employees and stakeholders.

They have a *stewardship mentality*—they know their investors and employees have taken a chance on them, and they want to prove them right. They are transparent, forthright, and don't play people like chess pieces: "Her desk sits right in the middle of the workspace. I never feel weird approaching her to ask a question, and she always takes the time to offer a thoughtful reply."

They are *positive*. They cultivate trust by being genuine, open, and honest. They're happy to admit that they're hopeful about the future. They also self-report that they're not particularly worried at the present moment. When they look at the world, they simply see more opportunities than threats.

In short, they are the chief cheerleader. This kind of attitude is crucial in a place where the future is often uncertain, and empowerment can often mean simply having the motivation to persevere through rough seas: "She is a joy to work with. She generates a team spirit—not an attitude of aloofness or superiority."

Why Founders Struggle to Work Through Others

No matter how brilliant your mind or strategy, if you're
playing a solo game, you'll always lose out to a team.
—Reid Hoffman and Ben Casnocha, *The Startup of You*[5]

We've just finished describing a group of people who are patient, composed, positive, approachable, supportive, and inclusive. To which a skeptical reader might respond: Is the answer to all my problems that I should "just be nice"? Is that all it takes to be successful?

To which we would respond: This same group of people has generated at least a 10x return on their investment dollars. They did not accomplish this by being shrinking violets. They did it by organizing effective collective effort. In fact, this same group of people actually *ranks low on empathy* (remember, they're founders), yet they are seen as sensitive and considerate. Why is that? Perhaps they are simply more aware of the need to listen and relate.

To explore the point further, let's take a look at the compositions of founders who struggle to work well with others. You will no doubt recognize some recurring themes.

All founders are self-confident, but these founders are particularly prone to displays of superiority and self-importance: "He uses other people's input as a way of strengthening his own argument—agreeing when it fits his own ideas, or trashing it when it doesn't." They humbly confess that their judgment about other people is almost always correct(!).

Not surprisingly, their 360 scores on judgment are in the tank. They don't listen, and they tend to talk *at* people, not with them: "Problems are used to call people out instead of bringing the team together." So they strangle innovation in the crib and kneecap their company's ability to scale: "He often calls for the team to take action for action's sake (ready, fire, aim), but these efforts are usually crippled by his own tendency to override everything."

But here we stumble into yet another paradox—these wild, free-thinking iconoclasts also happen to be incredibly *stubborn* and *rigid*. It's their way or the highway: "I have never seen him sincerely ask anyone for advice. Ever." Rich has heard it time and again: "It's just easier and quicker when I make the decisions." They insert themselves into meetings where they plainly lack context and depth of understanding, then they proceed to offer directives (or vague first impressions that are treated as directives). So they become the obstacle: "He has a tendency to question and override decisions made by others. Delegation becomes an exercise where tasks are completed on his behalf and employees feel like the managers of his personal tasks, rather than the supported owners of company goals."

How does this rigidity invariably manifest itself? As *micromanagement*, *mistrust*, and *miscommunication*: "The exec team is largely about optics and politics, and clearly no one trusts each other." People aren't sure what to do or how much authority they have, so they try to read the founder's mind (and that never ends well): "He thinks he's delegating, but he's actually just going through the motions. He does not explain to direct reports what he wants them to own and how they will measure success." The result is paralysis: "Throughout the organization, she is becoming seen more and more as a force that gets in the way of progress as opposed to a leader who empowers her team to succeed."

The Way Forward: Developing EQ

Here's when the breakdown typically happens: when the third layer arrives. That's when you no longer directly boss people around, but have to implement a middle-management layer. Most founders don't know how to manage, much less how to become a manager of managers. That's when the innate communication, the execution "by look and feel," suddenly evaporates. Then it all blows up: no one knows who owns what, nobody knows how to do their job, and everything becomes a game of telephone.

This is when you're hitting the limits of "Dunbar's number." The British anthropologist Robin Dunbar proposed that humans can comfortably maintain about 150 stable relationships, with closer relationships limited to around 5 to 15 people. After that, you need to start building a shared purpose. Why? Because startups don't exist. You can't find them in the wild. As *Sapiens* author Yuval Noah Harari points out, neither do religions or nation-states. They all depend upon our unique ability to build compelling narratives, shape common values, and build cohesive teams united behind a unifying vision.[6]

And to gain leverage by working through others, you need to develop your EQ. You need to cultivate the interpersonal skills that will allow you to connect with people, build trust, and maintain team cohesion. Rich estimates that 80% of his clients could use more EQ. When it comes to working through others, it's the "great differentiator." We have more relevant advice in the next section of the book, but here are a few places to start:

- **Listen actively:** Put the phone away. Make an effort to understand what others are saying without immediately thinking about your response.
- **Pause before reacting:** Give it a beat. When you feel a strong emotion, take a moment to pause and consider your response before acting.
- **Stay positive:** Cultivate a positive outlook and focus on what you can control rather than what you cannot.
- **Read a book or take a course:** *Emotional Intelligence* by Daniel Goleman offers a solid introduction.[7]
- **Ask for feedback:** Seek honest feedback from others about how you come across emotionally.

The founders who struggle to work well with others are often just as brilliant, creative, and visionary as their successful peers. But none of that matters, because they haven't been able to translate their ideas into collective action. They're far from lazy—most of them work themselves practically to death. But their efforts are hopelessly self-involved. They don't have the discipline and the focus (much less the humility) to motivate and organize a group of smart people to create something special. So, great ideas get lost in the tumult of reactivity and mismanagement. It's a tragedy.

Rich has had several clients who have bombed out on their first try, worked hard on their EQ, and succeeded the second time around. But we can't stress this enough—this is a *learned behavior*. Founders are never lacking in ideas; they're just generally deficient in the people skills necessary to translate those ideas into reality. EQ solves that problem.

CHAPTER 6

Systems and Execution: The Self-Driving Car

A founder comes out of a computer science program with the idea for a simple, intuitive telehealth app that organically takes the market by storm. After turning down an acquisition offer from Amazon (who tells him that he has a nice feature, but not a true stand-alone application on his hands), he finds himself sitting on lots of VC money with a mandate to turn his wildly popular app into a wildly profitable company. He's just out of school. He knows nothing about business. But now he's supposedly in charge of building one. So what does he do?

He goes back to what he knows. He knows he doesn't have the brash charisma or relentless assertiveness that many startup leaders are known for. Instead, he's a thoughtful, almost introverted leader who excels at building a few deep relationships and creating a culture of collaboration. He knows he built his app in his college dorm with the help of friends with similar personalities—bright, easygoing, somewhat disorganized, but relentlessly creative. Why not try to re-create that same environment in his new company?

So that's what he does. After an angel investor gives him enough to get started, he hires a small team of smart, genial kids fresh out of college, and he builds them the dorm of their dreams: free meals, game rooms, open bars, a nice gym, nap rooms, the whole works. And the initial idea takes off! The market really needs it. But its success creates an actual company with actual employees and actual customers, not to mention actual business needs: strategic goals, a product road map, a headcount plan, and so on.

The new company proceeds to accomplish absolutely nothing. Well, not exactly nothing—a few pet projects get shipped, but nothing really earth-shattering. His company is still coasting on the success of its first product. Meanwhile, the competition is ramping up. So he goes out and hires a tough, no-nonsense COO from Oracle, whom everyone proceeds to hate. It's not a surprise. These are young, laid-back nerds who don't appreciate getting barked at by a middle-aged man with a short temper. The COO resigns after six months. That's when the founder calls Rich.

Rich tells him that this is a textbook case of what happens when a person with a good idea who happens to be a natural Relationship Builder gets put in charge of an organization. "You're too worried about people liking you to hold them accountable," he tells him. "What's more, the culture you've built (which is entirely based on your own personality!) is inherently averse to top-down discipline. You're going to have to introduce execution into your organization through subtler means." Rich tells him that the company won't scale without efficient systems.

At first the founder rejects Rich's advice, calling structure, systems, and processes bureaucracy. Rich explains that it's about efficiency, not bureaucracy, unless you overdo it. Finally, he takes Rich's words to heart. He rolls out an OKR program, with lots of affable guest lecturers and plenty of support material. He frames the idea of a disciplined development process to his engineers as a tricky problem to solve, but one that can be done collaboratively and creatively. He works with his HR lead to backchannel and hire more "friendly" Managers of Execution across the entire organization.

Slowly but surely, the "execution transplant" operation begins to bear fruit. The creativity embedded in his organization becomes fused with focus and discipline. He wins the loyalty of customers by continually delighting them with new features and capabilities. He wins the loyalty of his team by empowering them with structure and accountability. He's still a nice guy, but now he's also someone who inspires people to build big things.

The Superhero Years

Most of the founders that Rich meets appear calm and focused. They might get a little anxious or excited, but for the most part, they seem healthy and lucid. Other times, however, they look like they haven't slept in weeks. They're plainly exhausted: drained faces, dazed looks in their eyes, stooped postures. They're crushed under the burdens of the world. Lots of times *it's the same founder*, before and after the first crush of real complexity hits.

When a startup is small, lurching from crisis to crisis is actually kind of fun. It's invigorating and energizing. You're a superhero solving problems, building a company, and creating value. But then the problems grow exponentially. So a situation that used to feel challenging but manageable suddenly devolves into a debilitating succession of 100-hour workweeks. Then all sorts of things get thrown out the window: personal agency, focused effort, rational problem-solving, affirming relationships, basic hygiene.

Rich remembers taking a long walk with one of these poor souls around Seattle. Rich asked him about his personal life (none). He asked him about the last time he dated someone (years ago). He asked him about his outside interests (none). He asked him about the last book he read (quizzical facial expression).

Both Rich and Tien have been there. They immensely enjoyed their superhero years, when their companies were nice and small and the world was a much simpler place. They had complete situational awareness. They could boss people around. If something felt out of whack, they could shoot a text or call a quick huddle, and things would quickly move in the direction they wanted. But at some point, they hit a wall. Why did this happen? Because they didn't build the systems needed to help their companies scale.

You'll know it when things start to really come undone. You'll hear statements like "The left hand doesn't know what the right hand is doing." Your culture scores will start to tank. The Glassdoor ratings will complain about how management sits in an ivory tower. The questions will come hard and fast: Why did the sales team say that? Why didn't the customer support rep just reach out to this engineer and quickly solve the customer's problem? Why has this important decision just been festering for weeks, with no leader to jump in and make a call?

So the stress and anxiety descend, and the founder starts reverting to various default behaviors. Those are clear signs that the timer is counting down. Tick, tick, tick.

The old bad habits begin to assert themselves: "He doesn't set clear goals, doesn't follow through on the goals we do set." "He doesn't follow through on most of his product responsibilities, such as writing a spec or deciding about a feature." "He resists putting a line in the sand about which features we want to build by when. We're finally doing that, but way too late. Trying to do everything isn't a valid strategy." Et cetera, et cetera.

The Self-Driving Car

Why is being able to execute at scale so important? What is it about the personalities of founders that trips them up when it comes to actually producing results? How should they think about improving in this area?

To answer these questions, let's start with (you guessed it) a metaphor: the self-driving car. Tien uses this idea a lot when he talks to founders, and their eyes always light up. A car is a complex piece of machinery that we utterly take for granted. You turn the key (or push the button), step on the gas, turn the steering wheel, and suddenly you're moving through space. It might as well be magic—but it's not. It's actually an impressive piece of engineering.

Now, let's consider a self-driving car. Talk about magic and wizardry! The engineering challenges involved are astounding. The vehicle has to anticipate an endless series of scenarios. It's taken over a decade of field testing just to get these things puttering around some designated cities and suburbs. But they're coming. Pretty soon, they'll be everywhere.

You need a *system* in place to manage complexity—a single human being can't possibly handle all those moving parts. And what if that system looked something like a self-driving car? A system that is self-directing and self-organizing. Something that can essentially be left alone for a little while. You can take your hands off the wheel (maybe go lie prone in Hawaii for a week), but when you return, it'll still be essentially headed in the right direction. Of course, a few things will go wrong. They'll need to get fixed. But then the car will drive itself much better the next time you take your hands off the wheel.

If you are lucky or good or both, you will survive the initial phases of your startup's growth. But then—rest assured—a roaring tide of complexity will descend. And in order to negotiate that complexity, you're going to need to build a system that allows you to scale. You're going to need a collection of processes that combine to create something bigger than themselves, that create emergent properties that guide alignment. It sounds almost spooky, but then again, so are self-driving cars.

This is not an anecdotal observation. It's blatantly obvious when we examine the data. Looking at the competencies that differentiate successful and unsuccessful founders, we see a third cluster of competencies that are clearly correlated with each other, meaning, again, that successful founders tend to be good at all four of the skills below, and unsuccessful founders tend to be . . . the opposite.

- Results and productivity
- Taking initiative
- Developing structures, systems, and processes
- Reengineering processes

The picture is clear: Successful founders have learned the importance of aligning strategic objectives with systems and processes in order to execute at scale. Their unsuccessful peers have not.

Results and Productivity

These founders get results, accomplish objectives,
and see projects to completion.
—Rich Hagberg

Some founders are mercurial. They have a "holistic" approach to getting things done (in other words, they don't). They love thinking about problems, but once they feel they've arrived at a solution in their head, they get bored and move on. They can't be bothered to finish their homework.

It's a lot like the marathon racers who hit the 22-mile mark and then say to themselves: "Meh. I know I can finish this thing, so why bother," and then quit to go enjoy the sunset. Or the CTO who finishes whiteboarding an architecture plan, then considers their job finished without writing a line of code (true story—Tien worked with someone like this). It's the founder who loves telling the story, repeating the vision, seeing the possibilities, but then doesn't stress out if the product isn't shipped or the numbers aren't met.

Alfred Hitchcock famously said that every one of his movies was completed before he shot a roll of film, because they were scripted and storyboarded so thoroughly. But then again, *he did go on to shoot the movie.*

Execution-minded leaders don't rest until the goal is accomplished: the product is shipped, the customer is live, the weekly average users exceed the target we set, we make the top right quadrant, etc. That's why successful founders tend to be rated much higher on results and productivity than unsuccessful founders.

Founders who excel in this area are exceptionally *focused.* They simply don't stop until the job is done. They have a "stick-to-itiveness" that makes them congenitally unable to leave a project unfinished. Their colleagues rate them high on dependability (0.7 standard deviations above the mean), whereas they rate their less successful peers much lower (1.6 standard deviations below the mean on average).

To make sure their priorities are translated into clear goals, these founders establish a disciplined planning process. They recognize that priorities on their own aren't enough—everyone must have a clear set of goals that contribute to those priorities. For the car to run itself, all the individual systems need to have a specific purpose.

The objective is to reduce ambiguity, create alignment, and get people hyperfocused on hitting goals and getting things done. This requires continual communication about priorities, goals, and milestones. It entails following up and tracking progress. And it ultimately means emphasizing actual results over valiant efforts.

And perhaps even more importantly, these priorities tell them what *not* to do. There are only so many hours in the day: "She is very good about sharing her to-dos daily and longer term and updating the team as those items get completed. Although there are a number of goals that change over time due to incomplete information, she is great about Level A setting."

Taking Initiative

These founders make clear-cut decisions without unnecessary delay, even in tough situations.
—Rich Hagberg

Why is taking initiative so important to scalable execution? Well, start-ups are a complex endeavor. They move fast, they involve a lot of uncertainty, the competition can be fierce, and individuals can have an outsized impact. In this context, one of the most critical aspects of successful founders is their ability to proactively identify problems and implement effective solutions.

In fact, we see comment after comment that praise their vigilance in recognizing inefficiencies and recurring problems before they escalate. The key part here is "before they escalate." Their less successful peers often wait until systems completely collapse or inefficiencies become near fatal before taking action. They tend to react to problems rather than proactively addressing them. As a result, they compound problems and incur all sorts of opportunity costs in the process.

The founders who swim against this tide are *organized* and *orderly*. They are happy to note that they hate messy desks. Their structured approach allows them to identify issues systematically and address them promptly. Their patience and deliberate nature further enhance their ability to implement well-considered solutions rather than hastily executed fixes that might not stand the test of time: "In operational meetings, he can cut to the chase and ask the right kinds of questions to identify potential issues. He's really good at using his team to find the correct solution."

As a result, they are *proactive*. They are champions of speed, efficiency, and responsiveness. They are eternally vigilant when it comes to recognizing inefficiencies. This approach ensures continuous improvement and positions the company to handle increased demand and complexity as it grows: "She is intellectually curious about all parts of the business and has been able to identify problems before other members of the team have."

They hold themselves *accountable*. They create a culture of responsibility and excellence. Their team members note that these founders are not only good at identifying organizational flaws but are also willing to take decisive action to address them. Their leadership inspires others to take initiative and contribute to problem-solving efforts. This trait is closely linked to their sense of obligation to meet stakeholder expectations and their willingness to do what is right (i.e., the Boy and Girl Scouts stuff).

Finally, they are *guided by data*. Stakeholders note that these founders are adept at using information to inform their strategies and track the impact of process changes. This approach ensures that initiatives are based on reliable information, leading to more accurate goal setting and higher productivity. Having the data tell you what you need to fix really pushes you to take initiative.

Developing Structures, Systems, and Processes

These founders design and establish structures, systems, and processes to most effectively achieve the organization's objectives.
—Rich Hagberg

Walk into any Starbucks anywhere in the world, and you know what the basic physical experience is going to be: the smell of coffee, the banter of baristas, a comfortable chair. At the same time, you have modularity and autonomy. You can order a specialty drink that involves 18 exotic modifications.

When you walk into the first Starbucks in Pike Place in Seattle, however, it looks nothing like the others you've seen. You can see Schultz being inspired by the place. But how do you get from there to 30,000 locations?

That took a systems specialist. Someone who was able to abstract what made the first Starbucks special, and then re-create it at a mass scale. Similarly, Netflix is all over the world, but it still offers all kinds of modularity and culturally tailored products. There are famously as many Netflix home screens as there are Netflix users.

How did Reed Hastings and Howard Schultz do it? Like Henry Ford or Ray Kroc or Michael Dell, they recognized that *systems are not bureaucracy*. They understand that when administered effectively, formal processes help speed things up, not slow them down. Systems help them capitalize on opportunities as they try to reach new markets while also maintaining a compelling customer experience. As a result, every single one of their core business functions has a guiding analytic infrastructure.

They each built their own self-driving cars. They figured out how to build a system that takes dollars or people on one side and outputs desired outcomes (customer experience, revenue, growth, fired-up workforce, fame and fortune) on the other side. It drives itself. You just need to give it some gas. In many ways, once you get initial traction, your job as the founder/CEO is to build that system!

Now, just like Howard Schultz needed Orin Smith, or like Steve Jobs needed Tim Cook, or like Drew Houston needed Dennis Woodside, you don't have to go it alone. But you have to appreciate the need for systems. That's why successful founders who have demonstrated they can deliver execution at scale tend to have the following characteristics.

They value *order*. As a result, they are generally less manic. Less anxious. More patient. They self-report that they do not feel like they have to keep consistently on the move. They also state that they don't worry much about the future. As we'll discuss later in the book, these founders are simply much more *grounded*. While all founders are rebels and nonconformists, these people have *a general respect for structure and authority* that unsuccessful founders lack.

They are also *systems thinkers*. They can see order out of chaos and simplify a complex concept into component parts. They have an uncanny, Spock-like capacity to approach problems methodically, analyze data, and derive sound conclusions: "She has this amazing ability to stop time and really sit with a problem and consider it critically." They are logical.

They are constantly *weighing structure against flexibility*. This is admittedly a very tricky balancing act. To quote Eric Ries: "Companies that insist on building a world-class infrastructure before shipping a product are doomed to 'achieve failure,' because they're starved of feedback for too long . . . On the other hand, companies that take a 'just do it' attitude without any process at all are also taking a major gamble."[1] In Rich's experience, it's very rare to see a founder who places *too much* emphasis on structure. When the company starts to really take off, you're probably better off over-indexing on systems versus flexibility.

Ultimately, these founders understand that systems don't just support their business—they *are* their business. To quote Michael Gerber: "Systems run the business and people run the systems. People come and go but the systems remain constant."[2] Without them, there's no insight. There's no way to streamline operations and minimize mistakes. There's simply no way to measure what's working and what isn't: "He has the clearest understanding of the company and processes so he is able to lead these types of initiatives very well."

Re-Engineering Processes

> *These founders identify inefficiencies and recurring problems and restructure the organization to maximize effectiveness.*
> —Rich Hagberg

Creating new systems isn't enough. Why? Because you never get it right the first time. As you scale, things inevitably start to fall apart. Startups are in a constant state of flux—because they're growing so fast, or entering a new region, or disrupting a legacy market with a new idea. Everything is new and uncertain. All the playbooks have a half-life of usefulness.

Successful founders *constantly challenge their existing systems.* They are always looking for successful patterns to replicate. They press their team to conduct postmortems, so problems don't repeat themselves. They are relentless optimizers: "He is constantly interrogating our infrastructure to make sure it will get us where we need to go."

They are *never satisfied.* They sweat the last detail, the last mile. Like Jobs, they famously "paint the inside of the fence." That being said, they're not reactive or impulsive. They establish their golden metrics first, and then they figure out the tactics needed to get them there. They have a strategic and methodical approach to improving things that emphasizes simplicity: "He is very insightful in establishing the most simple yet productive methodology in systems and processes."

They also appreciate a *certain amount of routine.* They may not relish attending a weekly product meeting, but they recognize that if things get left unchecked, entropy might take over. They are constantly urging their team to work smarter. They might not know everything about a given system (nor should they), but they know who's responsible for it, and they make sure it's on the agenda—that it's being sourced and developed correctly. They take the time to step back and consider new ways to improve things.

They may have different frameworks—Kaizen, Six Sigma, the Five Whys—but these founders live by a process of continual improvement. Why? Because they understand that most organizations do not rise to the level of their goals but rather fall to the level of their systems.

How Founders Struggle with Execution

Founders tend to view formal structures and processes [...] as bureaucratic threats to their entrepreneurial souls. They also worry about losing speed, control, and team intimacy. When they eschew order and discipline, however, they pay a steep price: chaotic operations and unpredictable performance.
—Ranjay Gulati and Alicia DeSantola, "Start-Ups That Last," *Harvard Business Review*[3]

Unsuccessful founders score three standard deviations lower on execution than successful ones. It's a huge differentiator. These founders are generally disorganized and disorderly. They're not big on planning or structure. Their general motto is "Don't fence me in." They prefer spinning up new ideas rather than maintaining existing systems. They would much prefer to off-load problems than implement solutions.

Their general inability to collaborate tends to result in hopelessly frag-mented work efforts. They're happy to whiteboard the afternoon away while their company is drowning in stress and dysfunction. They're fiddling while Rome burns.

Of course, lots of founders struggle with infrastructure primarily because they don't know much about it. It's very difficult to implement a completely foreign concept: "He clearly doesn't have the experience to know what to do about it." The founders who have previously worked for larger organizations may have more experience with systems, but it's dif-ficult to translate sophisticated enterprise solutions into the context of a startup team. So they might appreciate systems in theory, but they're actu-ally pretty hopeless when it comes to their practical application.

All these issues mostly stem from their own deep-seated dysfunctions. Just like in a horror movie, the call is coming from inside the house.

These people are inherently *disorderly, unsystematic, haphazard,* and *messy.* All four of those adjectives come straight from the analysis of their personality profiles. They are fine with disorganization and chaos. In fact, they often seem to prefer it: "He is very inefficient and unorganized and seems to be quite comfortable with it. I have seen him spend lots of time looking for stuff on his hard drive. He is not methodical and rarely puts in place timelines or clarifies due dates."

Unfortunately, the mad scientist approach simply doesn't work when it comes to managing large organizations. Imagine hundreds of people rummaging around your bombed-out desk, looking for answers: "She is generally anti-structure/process and often counteracts any attempt by other members of the management team to create any."

They *don't respect rules*. Of course, *all* founders tend to hate rules, but successful founders acknowledge that they at least have a place. They serve a function. Their counterparts, however, *hate* them—they score well below average on general conformity. They react to a statement like "I respect rules because they guide me" with absolute antipathy. As a result, they frequently take the whole "break things, fail fast" ethos to its grim, logical conclusion.

Surprise, surprise—they're also not considered *dependable*. Even when they try to build systems, they don't finish the job. The result is inconsistent implementation. Everything is ad hoc. Temporary solutions are left to wither on the vine: "Attempts have been made, but there's been no follow-through, no accountability for enforcing the processes that are put in place." The mortality statistics are grim: "The structures, systems, and processes don't tend to last beyond a quarter."

But eventually, growth will outpace the development of the systems you need to (a) succeed and (b) stay sane in the process. The company is being forced to run when it hasn't even learned to walk correctly. Things fall apart. The center cannot hold. So founders, true to form, overreact and micromanage. They parachute in and try to fix things, with predictable results: "He scheduled a design and engineering meeting for a time when the lead designer wasn't available, prioritizing his own involvement over the entire team." Or they disengage and simmer with resentment: "Not very good at structure. Relies on other people to succeed based on their own ways of figuring things out."

They *don't empower their people*. Their successful peers try to answer simple questions: "Does everyone understand our priorities? Do they have what they need to do their jobs? Do they have the information they need to make good decisions? What key obstacles are they facing?" When Tien is dealing with a team whose work he isn't particularly familiar with, one of his go-to questions is: "If there was one thing I could do to help make your job easier, what would it be?"

Instead, these founders centralize all the decision-making and wind up becoming huge bottlenecks: ""He will from time to time do a 'deep dive' on a particular area of distress and ultimately will brute force a fix. If instead he empowered his e-team to lead and drive these efforts (and held them accountable for doing so), it would make for better organization harmony and scalability."

As a result, they are *burned out.* They constantly complain about their lack of energy and inability to concentrate. All the self-inflicted stress has ransacked their frontal cortex. They're utterly debilitated because they haven't built the systems they need to negotiate complexity and achieve results. Minor problems are constantly hijacking their attention: "His expectations are high, which is great, but he seems out of touch with the reality that it will take to get there. The company continually misses large initiatives due to too much attention dedicated toward smaller and less important projects."

It's not a surprise! They haven't put the systems in place, so they're forced to drag the entire project uphill all by themselves. It's like some horrible Greek tragedy. They're strung out all over the place, with little to show for their efforts: "He seems permanently distracted. I can't get any priorities out of him. It's no wonder we're so buried."

The Way Forward

There's a detailed advice chapter on systems and processes in the next section of the book, but the main message is this: If you suck at execution, it's okay. You'll probably never be great at it, but you should try to improve anyway.

Here are four things to concentrate on:

- **Clean your desk (whatever that "desk" happens to be):** Personal organization provides organizational clarity. Without it, you can't identify issues, organize efforts, and achieve results.
- **Respect systems:** Understand why your company needs them. Recognize that without them, you'll never be able to scale. You'll stall out.

- **Hire great execution people:** Ideally, they should have *already experienced* your next two to three years of planned growth. They'll have much better context.
- **Think of your organization as a product:** This is particularly relevant if you are an engineer or a technical type. Then you'll appreciate the complexity. Your natural instincts will kick in. Just remember that people aren't code.

At the end of the day, your job is to build a system that works without you. Your job is to build a self-driving car.

CHAPTER 7

Personal Grounding: The Rock in the Stream

This founder can't figure it out. The world used to feel like it was full of ideas and opportunities, but now all she sees are threats and potential catastrophes. Her e-commerce software company has lost some big clients. Delivery schedules have slipped. Some early employees have left in a huff. The storm clouds are starting to pile up.

As the issues multiply, she becomes a black cloud. Strategy meetings are particularly fraught. Admitting she is wrong on any point is a challenge she rarely overcomes. Her team has plenty of ideas, but no one feels like risking their heads if she hears something she doesn't like. They become very practiced at walking on eggshells. The board inevitably calls Rich.

The founder admits to Rich that she hates the idea of not being in control. She knows it's not sustainable, but she fixates on everything that can go wrong. She also knows she is overcommitted, extended beyond her limits, and that her impatience is palpable to everyone around her. But isn't that what all founders are like?

Rich introduces her to a very simple concept: cognitive reframing. "Stress is the water that founders swim in," he says. "Anxiety, self-doubt, and emotional exhaustion are all part of the job. You can either use that stress to build resilience and personal grounding, or let it overwhelm you." To quote John Milton: "The mind is its own place, and in itself can make a heaven of hell, a hell of heaven."

The task is to engage in some mental jujitsu. To reframe crisis as opportunity. To turn pressure into motivation. To channel perfectionism into a keen focus on steady progress. To look at harsh criticism as potentially valuable information. To recognize uncertainty as an occasion for flexibility and innovation. To acknowledge breaking points as the inevitable byproducts of growth. To rediscover the positive, creative mindset you had when you were just getting started as an ambitious young founder.

For example:

- The product is starting to get trashed on social media, so this is an opportunity to learn what went wrong and improve. Determine the biggest issues, then get to work resolving them.
- There's uncertainty in the market, so this means there are all kinds of opportunities for agility and innovation. What's more, *you* get to control how quickly you adapt and respond.
- Your competitor got a big new funding round, so this shows there's strong market interest. Use the news to help you to focus on your unique strengths and continue innovating.
- Yes, you're working ridiculously hard now, but it won't always be this intense. These early stages are critical for building momentum. The hard work you're putting in now is an investment in the future of the company.
- You don't have all the resources you need, so let necessity become the mother of invention. Figure out how to become more creative and lean.

Slowly but surely, the founder begins to flip the script. She gradually begins to shift her perspective from defeatism and frustration to a constructive, growth-oriented attitude. Then she puts plans and processes in place around this new mindset. Lo and behold, the smaller issues begin to evaporate (as it turns out, they weren't that important to begin with). And the larger issues become much more tangible and manageable.

Her team increasingly looks to her as someone they can count on. As a source of stability and equanimity. As a rock in the river. As a leader who looks at a challenge and says: "I'm not worried. We'll make it work. This is only going to make us better. We just need to focus and pull together."

Startups are directly hazardous to your mental and physical health, potentially resulting in anxiety, depression, insomnia, weight gain or loss, sexual dysfunction, substance abuse, you name it. There's a reason why startup researchers study high-stress environments like trauma centers and inpatient clinics.

Of course, it doesn't start off that way. In the early days, things are fun and exciting. If you're actually able to ship a product and land a few customers, there's suddenly all sorts of new information and insights to explore. There are sharp new people to hire.

But then those people wind up having equally sharp opinions. As do your customers, your investors, and your engineers. And suddenly you find yourself standing in the middle of a room full of sharp people offering sharp opinions. Just being able to maintain your sanity in this kind of environment is an accomplishment.

A select few, however, are blessed to have the emotional resilience to maintain their discipline and focus amid all this tumult. They're not perfect, but they are simply much better at recognizing their worst impulses and making an honest effort to account for them. They have more awareness at the moment, in the heat of battle, and can monitor their impulses and adjust their behavior accordingly.

They might get mad at someone, but they try to avoid making things worse by sending a flaming email. They may think of something sharp to say, but they'll hold their tongue. When they have a big decision to make amid a ransacked schedule and a million priorities, they'll clear space, make time, gather input, and think deliberately.

Even the best occasionally fall prey to outbursts, burnout, and reactive decisions, but they are simply much better than others when it comes to living in the middle of a cyclone. They are simply more balanced individuals; they are closer akin to a boulder in a raging river.

But most of us aren't. So what can we do about it?

Personal Grounding

The final differentiating cluster between successful and unsuccessful founders, which we call *personal grounding*, contains four correlated competencies:

- Sound judgment and reasoning
- Resilience and stress management
- Forthrightness
- Model of values

In essence, being *personally grounded* is about having a solid foundation of emotional and moral stability that guides one's actions and decisions, particularly in challenging or stressful situations. This trait is marked by a balanced approach to life, a strong ethical framework, and the ability to maintain composure and clarity under pressure. We've all known these kinds of people. They mostly teach through their actions.

What's another way of describing personal grounding? Good mental health, plain and simple. Being grounded increases your feelings of overall well-being, reduces anxiety and fear, and helps maintain perspective. It gives founders sound judgment—they can consider different viewpoints without obsessing about things they can't control. It also helps them be more open to learning, let go of control, and empower people through better, healthier relationships.

Crucially, founders with strong personal grounding understand that, like it or not, everyone is watching. They recognize the influence they have on the people around them. They know that when you are in a leadership role, there are no trivial acts. Everything you do makes a speech. They understand that leaders need to provide steady and consistent guidance and be models of responsible behavior.

All companies, no matter how successful, go through difficult times. They all have their near-death experiences. These might make great war stories later, but they're certainly not much fun in the moment. That's when you need the rock in the river, the source of gravity in the room that empowers everyone to focus and execute.

It also gives them integrity, which is really important. If you don't have integrity, you *will* be found out. It's essential for building trust, enhancing credibility, fostering accountability, and promoting ethical behavior. Rich's database of personality traits and 360 ratings is loud and clear on this issue: Integrity plays a pivotal role in creating a positive organizational culture and ensuring sustainable growth.

All founders have healthy egos. It comes with the job. The problem is that they have dozens of people doing their very best to inflate those egos on a daily basis. Any confident person could fall prey to their worst impulses in that situation. Grounded founders have learned how to identify and avoid those traps.

Let's explore how personally grounded founders shape the culture of their organizations.

Judgment and Reasoning

These founders effectively diagnose problems, identify core issues, exercise common sense, see critical connections and ramifications, and analyze alternatives.
—Rich Hagberg

Strictly from a physiological perspective, startup environments are a disaster when it comes to making sound decisions. When we were early humans, brief but emphatic general discharges of our sympathetic nervous systems helped us avoid danger and escape predators. Today, we're not struggling for survival on the veldt anymore, but no one has told our nervous systems.

Far too many founders suffer from chronic stress, which is more or less a permanent state of low-level "fight-or-flight" response. A limbic system that's flooded with stressors plays havoc with our decision-making capabilities. As Stanford neurologist Robert Sapolsky explains:

> What does chronic stress do to the frontal cortex? Atrophy of neurons, disconnecting circuits. As a result, you make the most idiotic decisions, which are going to haunt you for the rest of your life, and yet you think they're brilliant at the time. That's another effect of chronic stress: your judgment goes down the tubes.[1]

What a cruel fate. At the same time that you are being forced to constantly context shift within a small, inexperienced team, your frontal cortex (which controls things like self-discipline, long-term planning, and emotional regulation) is being fried like an egg. By definition, every decision you make in a startup is going to be based on incomplete information. You only need to make a single bad "bet the company" call for everything to go south.

Amid all this craziness, grounded founders are much more *reflective and deliberate*. On their personality tests they may indicate a sense of urgency, but they are not impulsive. They score higher on personality attributes like Planful, Patient, and Disciplined. At the same time, they're not overly complex thinkers; they see themselves as fairly straightforward people.

They self-report that they rarely do anything reckless. They are more grounded in the facts and better at listening to alternatives before acting: "He does a great job of distancing himself from all the day-to-day stuff so that he can consider big systemic decisions as opposed to jumping on immediate issues. He's figured out how to focus on the truly important material."

These founders are lauded for their ability to make well-informed decisions *based on thorough analysis and understanding of the situation*. They are much more disciplined about gathering feedback and considering alternate paths. They rank high on personality test items like Team-Oriented and Seeks Support and Advice: "He considers lots of angles before making a big call."

Rich remembers when a founder proposed an exciting new strategic initiative to his executive team, to which his head of IT responded, "My department is still overwhelmed by integrating the software systems of two recent acquisitions, and if we try to do this right now it will break the back of my organization." The founder got the message and postponed the new initiative until the next year. He simply had more situational awareness.

These founders are particularly adept at *identifying core issues*. They don't waste their time on minor inconveniences. They rank high on personality items like Systematic and Strategic. They can think structurally and understand the broader implications of their decisions and actions: "She is great at identifying the biggest shark in the water and going after it."

They are also recognized for their *problem-solving skills*. They win high marks for their ability to think analytically and logically: "She's always trying to find the best solution, regardless of politics and ego. She does a great job of breaking down complex problems into individual parts and then engaging them methodically." But they can also turn on their collective influencing skills after they've made their decision.

Here's Peter Drucker, the godfather of management:

> They try to find the constants in a situation, to think through what is strategic and generic rather than to "solve problems." They are, therefore, not overly impressed by speed in decision-making; rather, they consider virtuosity in manipulating a great many variables a symptom of sloppy thinking. They want to know what the decision is all about, and the underlying realities which it has to satisfy. They want impact rather than technique. And they want to be sound rather than clever.[2]

Resilience and Stress Management

These founders cope well with the stress and the demands of the job, maintaining energy, strength, and endurance. They rebound quickly from setbacks and persevere in the face of adversity.
—Rich Hagberg

Startups are practically designed to dismantle your emotional control. A founder is always expected to project confidence, even when they're melting down internally. The dissonance takes a toll. As Sam Altman writes: "There is a huge amount of pressure as a founder to never show weakness and to be the cheerleader in all internal and external situations. The world can be falling down around you—and most of the time when you're running a company, it is—and you have to be the strong, confident, and optimistic one. Failing is terrifying, and so is looking stupid."[3]

Resilient founders are generally seen as *secure and stable*. They don't have mood swings (or at least visible ones): "It takes a lot to get her angry. I've rarely seen her raise her voice, even when she's arguing in favor of something she feels strongly about." They rank high on personality items like Deliberate and Practical; they seem to have an inner damping function. They generally agree with the statement: "Emotion rarely causes me to act without thinking."

In response to all the pressure, they simply do a better job of "keeping it together." They score high on personality items like Composed, Calm, and Introspective. They self-report that they are almost always able to keep their emotions in control, which may not be completely accurate(!), but they are far less prone to tantrums and destructive outbursts of anger: "It takes a lot to rattle her. She is very centered and takes a long-term view of things. She is a rock, and even when she is stressed, she keeps her cool."

Resilient founders seem to do a much better job of *applying conscious thought to their emotions before responding*. Although they are very far from being warm, fuzzy therapists, their awareness of their own emotions makes them more understanding of the ups and downs of others. They are particularly effective at emotional mirroring, or the ability to understand and reflect back the emotions of others. As discussed in chapter five, "Working Through Others," they are simply much more socially adroit, diplomatic, and empathetic. As the Cambridge psychologist Simon Baron-Cohen notes: "Empathy is like a universal solvent. Any problem immersed in empathy becomes soluble."[4]

Like all founders who excel at working with others in stressful situations, they are *positive*. This isn't the same thing as vapidly optimistic. They're genuinely confident and hopeful. They self-report that they make an effort to see the best in every situation. They also don't mind it when other people occasionally laugh at their mistakes. They are seen as much more likely to bounce back from adversity: "The last 18 months have been a wild ride, but I'm amazed by her ability not just to stay balanced, but stay excited. Her positive attitude is infectious."

Finally, *they do not give up*. They endure. They persevere. They keep attacking a problem until it's fixed. They have a capacity for punishment that leaves their colleagues slack-jawed: "The level of stress he's been under at times is crazy, but most of the team has absolutely no idea of that, because he hardly shows it unless you look very closely. He works like a dog and seems to bounce back quickly from long stretches of work and stress."

Forthrightness

These founders are sincere, genuine, open, and direct
with others. They have no hidden agenda.
—Rich Hagberg

Forthright founders are significantly more comfortable than their peers when it comes to openly expressing a range of emotions. They are less likely to be viewed as having secret intents. Crucially, this creates trust, something that takes lots of time to build but a minimal amount of effort to destroy. Trust pays all sorts of dividends. Like Ben Horowitz says in *The Hard Thing About Hard Things*:

> As a company grows, communication becomes its biggest challenge. If the employees fundamentally trust the CEO, then communication will be vastly more efficient than if they don't. Telling things as they are is a critical part of building this trust. A CEO's ability to build this trust over time is often the difference between companies that execute well and companies that are chaotic.[5]

Of course, there's no such thing as complete transparency in any organization. But these founders share as much information as possible. They tell it like it is. They're straight with their employees: "She is sincere, genuine, open, and direct with others. She does not have a hidden agenda." They rank high on Openness and Honesty. As a result, they create reciprocal relationships, not one-way directives. This is especially important as a company grows and its founder simply isn't physically around as much.

In the early years, Google founders Larry Page and Sergey Brin were famously honest about the state of their business with their employees (granted, they mostly had excellent news to share). They held regular all-hands meetings called "TGIF" (Thank God It's Friday), where they discussed company performance, answered employee questions, and shared details about revenue, challenges, and future plans.

Transparency breeds respect: "His personal honesty has never, ever been in question. There is absolutely no doubt about his sincerity. It is a central part of why I decided to join the company."

Model of Values

> *These founders engender respect from others through consistent moral and ethical behavior, high standards of personal conduct, and promoting and modeling the principles and values that are central to the success of the organization.*
> —Rich Hagberg

Integrity is often described as doing the right thing, even when no one is watching. In a startup, everyone is watching. Unfortunately, that doesn't make being a good person any easier—far from it. The pressures can be a huge test of your moral and ethical boundaries. You need to know where the line is and not step over it.

Think of all the temptations involved in such a crushingly stressful environment: exaggerating the traction of your business when fundraising, infringing on a competitor's IP when developing a competitive product, or exploiting your customer data when you're looking for new revenue streams. The opportunities to let your morals slide are endless, and if you're not careful, they can land you in court. One person's example of blatant deceit is another person's version of "fake it until you make it."

We're all familiar with the names of founders who succumbed to these temptations (we mentioned a few of them at the beginning of the book). But again, be careful before you caricature these people as pure villains. At another time, in another startup, with another several hundred million dollars, you might also be tempted to cut some corners.

The founders who rank high on Model of Values *demonstrate consistency between words and actions*: "He communicates as much by how he acts as what he says." They recognize that stated company values are window dressing if they don't reflect actual behavior and practices. They understand that the reputation and credibility of the founder can make or break a company's brand.

They are seen as *honest*. They don't prevaricate or obfuscate. They tell it like it is, even when the news is difficult: "He consistently demonstrates honesty in his dealings, never shying away from admitting mistakes and always providing clear and accurate updates." As the entrepreneur Bret Waters puts it:

> My recommendation for startup founders is to be in the habit of telling the truth. This means that sometimes you'll be telling customers and investors things they don't want to hear, but by doing so, you'll be building trust that will serve you well in the long run. You'll also be establishing the right tribal culture for your team. A team built around values of honesty, transparency, and long-term decision-making will always outperform a team run by a CEO who is in the habit of telling lies for short-term gain. "A fish rots from the head down," the saying goes.[6]

These founders demonstrate a *fundamental respect for others*. They see themselves as stewards, not rock-star CEOs. They rank high on Sensitivity and Consideration, Relationship Building, and Listening. They embody a sense of servant leadership.

Selfless leaders, perhaps counterintuitively, wind up being indispensable. When you lose them, you risk losing the company: "She is a total master when it comes to our values and to our strategy. She is the bedrock of this company." In contrast, when a board fires a self-obsessed founder, the procedure is relatively painless. Nobody minds, since they were never particularly attached to or trusted by the people in the organization in the first place. They've made themselves *easy* to replace.

How Founders Struggle with Personal Grounding

A lack of personal grounding turns all your potential positives into outright negatives. It turns a founder's drive and charisma into entitlement and narcissism. It turns a commanding presence into a facade that hides the insecurity that fuels the imposter syndrome. It turns a will to shape the universe into a "fake it until you make it" mentality where lies and obfuscations prevail. It flips persuasion into manipulation, where empathy and ethical considerations are secondary to winning your own personal blue ribbon.

A willingness to bend rules and ethical lines might be part of your renegade, tradition-busting style, but when there's no moral compass, it signals a profound lack of internalized social and ethical standards. Confidence and risk-taking go hand in hand with the "entrepreneurial spirit," but without sound judgment, it turns into recklessness at best and willful blindness at worst: "I appreciate the positive attitude, but it can sometimes come across as completely clueless. There are a lot of competitors in our space, and surely not *all of them* suck."

Without authentic self-confidence and integrity, the courage of conviction devolves into knee-jerk defensiveness, a reluctance to seek help for fear of appearing weak or vulnerable. A strong bias for action turns into impatience and impulsivity that ransacks effective judgment. Difficulty forming strong attachments might be the result of lots of churn and turnover, but without empathy and compassion, it could represent a deep-seated fear of vulnerability.

As we'll explore further, a lack of personal grounding also attacks one of a founder's deepest vulnerabilities, their sense of self-awareness. It destroys introspection, self-reflection, and the ever-constant struggle against mental bias. When founders lack the ability to spot their own bullshit, then havoc ensues: "He quickly turns defensive when handling constructive criticism, and his default mode seems to be 'high-school debate team.'"

For founders, who even on their best days have a deep-seated aversion to conflict and a strong desire to be liked, a lack of authentic confidence results in avoidance, passive-aggressiveness, and dysfunction. These founders confess on their personality tests that they worry that others will take advantage of them. This is usually because they haven't initially set boundaries, clearly laid out their expectations, or confronted behavior that was clearly out of line. Because they lack the courage to say what they really think, the problems only proliferate, and everyone loses.

Founders are generally outgoing people. But when they are not grounded, they often turn inward. Their lack of conviction undermines their independence and self-worth. They admit that they worry excessively about what people will think of them, but they're afraid to speak out. They constantly crave approval, but they can't assert themselves. They throw themselves into fits of analysis paralysis, overdoing consensus and compromise, turning everything into lowest-common-denominator decisions.

These founders self-report that they have an innate fear of being alone, so they surround themselves with people. But this doesn't seem to eliminate their feeling of isolation! They know how to fake sociability, but it's not real. Instead, they use their interpersonal skills to manipulate. They don't tell people what they really want and end up wallowing in resentment and acting passive-aggressively. Because they don't honestly communicate their real expectations and agenda, they don't get what they want, and their teams get stuck.

A lack of personal grounding turns determined mindsets into stubborn resistance to change, rigid thinking, and escalating interpersonal conflicts. Healthy skepticism and realism devolve into pessimism and cynicism, while a results-oriented focus degrades into unrealistic demands and insensitivity.

Low emotional intelligence plummets to zero, leading to trampled egos, hurt feelings, and burnout. Stoic equanimity morphs into a fear of failure, a need to control uncertainty, micromanagement, and perfectionism.

All founders struggle with control issues. Without authentic self-confidence and empathy, these issues transform into a toxic command-and-control attitude that disempowers and disengages people. An aversion to ambiguity solidifies into a perfectionism that stifles innovation and overlooks opportunities. Goal-oriented accountability deteriorates into a bitter stew of finger-pointing and risk aversion.

You see the general pattern here. You can't build anything without a foundation. Remove personal grounding, and minor conditions instantly transform into raging infections. It's important to identify your competency weaknesses and account for them, but if you're not a mature person, none of that effort will amount to anything. Everything is connected.

To illustrate, here is an absolute barn burner of a 360 review of a founder that Rich came across a few years ago:

> He is one of the worst managers I've ever had. He perpetually promises but does not deliver. He acts distant and comes off as inauthentic, removed, manipulative, and awkward. He actively avoids confrontation and does not communicate important thoughts he believes he will be challenged on (though he often produces frustration and a pressured environment in meetings and around the office). He routinely puts people down and demoralizes them. He treats his opinions as more important than others without substantiating them, and thus has extreme issues driving toward consensus. He frequently acts unprofessionally when meeting with people in person and does not have awareness when in a group social context. He is horrendous at planning and sticking to milestones and priorities. He is extremely bad at writing anything down to establish shared truth or accountability. He almost never shares company documents with the relevant people involved though demands that everyone share their documents/write-ups

with him. He often crosses personal boundaries such as contacting employees outside working hours for non–business critical reasons.

Notice how the emotional toxicity and the organizational chaos go hand in hand. These people simply lack a strong moral compass to ground their behavior. Something is missing inside them. They overpromise or exaggerate results, continually selling rather than telling the whole truth. They use their influencing skills to manipulate or take advantage of people. They simply think of themselves and often fail to consider the needs and concerns of others. Then they wonder why people don't seem to trust them, or why morale is so low around the office.

And it all catches up with them in the end.

The Way Forward

With the fading of characters like Neumann and Kalanick, the backslapping bro culture of Silicon Valley's aughts era is now seen as passé. Tech employees are self-aware enough not to be as openly misogynistic at their workplaces as some of Uber's employees were … But despite moves to austerity, today's founders' sensibilities remained largely the same. Like the managers of Uber and others before them, entrepreneurs proved willing to sidestep rules and take shortcuts to build the next potentially world-changing company.
—Mike Isaac, *Super Pumped: The Battle for Uber*[1]

There will always be founders who are expedient and prone to bending generally accepted moral principles if it is in their self-interest. There will always be founders who abuse power and engage in harmful behavior. There will always be people who have an easier time rationalizing away morally gray behaviors (and won't really value moral ethical standards in the first place).

So what's the way forward? Is integrity really a learned behavior? Can you teach a grown adult how to be a better person? After all, don't most of these people *know* they're acting out of line but decide to do it anyway?

Some do, and some don't. The people who don't want to be helped will meet their just rewards. But for those of you who want to do a better job of addressing your worst impulses, we can point you to a single concept: self-awareness.

It all starts with identifying the problem. Focus your attention internally on how you think and feel, and externally on how your behavior impacts others. Bringing a "watching presence" to everything you do will allow you to recognize patterns and pierce more deeply into who you are and what you experience. But the good news is that unlike integrity, self-awareness is very much a learned skill. And it can be applied to our moral architecture as well as our executive capacity.

That's not to say it's easy or straightforward. Self-awareness requires gaining perspective on your automatic pilot tendencies by recognizing them before spontaneously reacting. Self-awareness allows founders to be thoughtful, deliberate, and intentional in leading and making decisions. It also helps you deal with your coworkers and the challenges you will inevitably face together.

Most founders without personal grounding simply don't know themselves. They don't have a frame of reference. They either can't see, or they are willfully blind.

For founders, self-awareness is sight.

CHAPTER 8

Self-Awareness: Developing Personal Pattern Recognition

A sharp founder with a sales background comes up with a brilliant idea for a fintech platform that solves a major pain point for financial institutions—streamlining their backend operations to save time and money. His instincts are spot-on. Early success comes quickly. Investors take notice. Soon he's surrounded by an experienced team of executives—several have previously worked for big enterprise companies.

But he can't listen to them—either that, or he won't. This is particularly frustrating to his head of product, who is trying to get the company to stick with a product road map. He has done customer research and knows what customer trends are emerging and what engineering has prioritized. But when it comes to the founder's team or his customers, the customers are always right and the product strategy comes second. Remember, he's a sales guy. He wants to please everyone. So he says yes to every feature request or deal ask, driving his engineering and product teams crazy in the process. He becomes notorious for making up his mind and refusing to budge, even when his team or his board has valid concerns. Eventually, he gets referred to Rich.

Rich tells him that there's nothing wrong with him—he's a founder, he's headstrong. That's mostly a good thing, because there will be many more challenges ahead. He just needs to pair those headstrong instincts with self-awareness. He needs to build a truth machine, a system for counterbalancing his own biases with pragmatism and perspective.

He needs to understand that he has other important constituencies in addition to his customers—namely, his team. He needs to force himself into healthily uncomfortable situations by slowing down and seriously considering the informed opinions of others. Trying to please every customer will spread resources too thin and risk the success of the product. With a limited budget and engineering capacity, it's impossible to meet every demand, so success lies in making tough choices and investing where the most impact can be made. And making those kinds of decisions entails a self-awareness of your own personal biases.

Eventually, the founder and his team settle on an unspoken compromise—he's allowed to have his theatrics when it comes to confronting an opinion he doesn't like. But then . . . he goes away and counts to 10. He understands his bias is for decisive action, so he forces himself to listen to patient reasoning. He interrogates his instincts. Eventually, he comes around (well, most of the time).

Pragmatism prevails. The company succeeds. Everybody wins. An experienced executive team gets to apply a strategy to scale briskly but responsibly, and a founder gets to hang on to some minor theatrics.

As we've discussed, founders tend to be a mentally scattered group of people. Lost in the buzzing cloud of screamingly urgent priorities that constitute startup life, they quickly fall prey to the tyranny of the urgent. If they're not careful, they can exist in a kind of perpetually reactive hell. When their autopilot tendencies take over completely, they lose perspective.

The answer to this problem is *self-awareness*, or the ability to recognize our own patterns of thinking, behavior, and emotional reactions. It's an "aware presence" that gives you an observer-like perspective on yourself at the moment. It allows you to be aware of what is going on internally in your mind, viscerally in your body, and behaviorally in your actions. It also requires having a framework to understand the autopilot, reactive patterns that drive your thinking and actions. Self-awareness gives you the power to stop being a Ping-Pong ball that is controlled by your internal reactions and external circumstances. It's the essence of grounded leadership, and it has two primary categories of benefits: internal and external.

Internally, self-awareness is critical to overriding your own tendency to be distractible and avoiding the shiny-object syndrome that distracts founders and creates chaos in their organizations. It helps you to become more intentional and deliberate about your core values and monitor when your behavior might not be consistent with your moral and ethical standards. It helps you avoid reactivity and stay focused on what truly matters: What's truly important to me? What do I stand for? What am I feeling? What do I want? What are my goals? What am I good at? What am I trying to accomplish? What fears am I experiencing? What am I worried about? What am I frustrated about?

Externally, self-awareness helps you reflect and improve through interaction with others: How are people reacting to my behavior? How am I impacting the effectiveness of my team? Am I being too sharp? Am I focusing solely on problems and dysfunction? Am I forgetting to offer praise and positive reinforcement? Are people comfortable with sharing ideas around me? Am I seeking objective advice? Am I being deliberate with my own feedback? Am I helping others learn about themselves? Am I acting like a fundamentally decent human being?

If Rich were to sum up a critical part of his job as an executive coach in one sentence, it would be this: He helps founders develop self-awareness and use it to monitor their reactions, recognize their real motivations, and adjust their behavior. He does this because the data tells him this is a massive difference between success and failure. Without self-awareness, his clients will struggle to learn from what went well and what didn't and make the necessary adjustments. They won't be able to evolve.

If you can't recognize how you are reacting, you probably won't be able to take the necessary steps to adjust your behavior, and will ultimately cripple your company's chances for success. Watch out for spontaneity. The goal is to become an "intentional leader." As investor Anthony K. Tjan writes in a *Harvard Business Review* piece called "How Leaders Become Self-Aware":

Without self-awareness, you cannot understand your strengths and weaknesses, your "super powers" versus your "kryptonite." It is self-awareness that allows the best business-builders to walk the tightrope of leadership: projecting conviction while simultaneously remaining humble enough to be open to new ideas and opposing opinions. The conviction (and yes, often ego) that founders and CEOs need for their vision makes them less than optimally wired for embracing vulnerabilities or leading with humility. All this makes self-awareness that much more essential.[1]

The 360 comments of unsuccessful founders suggest that many of them have little awareness of their impact on others. They are absolutely clueless about their own behavior and how they affect people. They struggle to understand outside perspectives (and lots of them don't even try). They are dismissive, intimidating, and unapproachable. The worst seem to lack any sense of empathy. They're viewed as either being a robot, or an asshole, or some unfortunate combination of the two.

Lack of self-awareness hampers a founder's ability to manage the extreme demands of the job and their own emotions. Frustrations can easily build and build until the office supplies start flying. As another *HBR* piece called "How Founders Self-Destruct Under Pressure" describes:

Becoming increasingly aware of their stress-related behaviors and self-destructive patterns is increasingly important for entrepreneurs today, especially those who have never lived through an economic downcycle before. Self-awareness, paired with professional and personal support, can stave off self-destructive behaviors and pro-mote more positive interactions and, importantly, results.

    . . . An entrepreneur's optimism—there *is* a way, a solution *can* be found—is a positive trait when trying to launch a new business, albeit within reason. When it becomes unbridled, however, that optimism can turn to willful blindness about both the business-threatening forces that exist around them and the negative personality traits within them.[2]

We all have assets and liabilities, but when you become acutely and continuously aware of them, you can consciously choose the path that gives you a better chance to emerge victorious from the challenges of leading a company.

A direct report of one successful founder wrote, "He relishes receiving feedback and is highly adaptable. Has a creative approach to solving problems. There are few problems that he can't solve. He can exist in an ambiguous and unclear environment and yet see a path."

"He is very quick on his feet," wrote another reviewer. "He can adapt to changes quite easily and fast. He can get into a situation where people are panicking and bring order to their fears, it doesn't matter who is in the room. I have to internalize things and see how it fits in the big picture, but he seems able to do this in real-time."

The Dark Trinity of Poor Self-Awareness

Here's how poor self-awareness undermines your thinking, your emotions, and your behavior:

The Impact of Founder's Lack of Self-Awareness

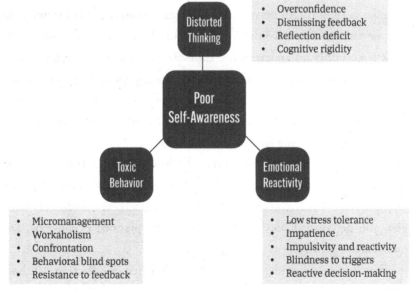

Self-Awareness and Distorted Thinking

A lack of self-awareness results in distorted and unexamined patterns of thinking. We all have habitual ways of seeing the world—entrenched mental biases coupled with a tendency to make snap judgments. Most founders are confident in their ability to assess their market, develop their product, manage their people, and generally decide what's important. But when that confidence lapses into outright arrogance, people lose their ability to recognize biases and consider other viewpoints. That's the opposite of thinking outside the box.

This kind of toxic overconfidence can also result in founders discounting valuable input from team members, advisors, or the market, leading to decisions based more on their personal convictions than on objective data. It can also prevent them from seeing potential flaws in their plans, increasing the risk of failure due to unchecked assumptions. Case in point: Adam Neumann, the cofounder of WeWork, emphasized rapid expansion over sustainable business practices.

While everyone values independent thinking, without self-awareness, it can degenerate into a stubborn resistance to considering other ideas and approaches. It can lead founders to ignore proven methods and reject sound advice that doesn't necessarily align with their vision. As a result, they're left isolated from useful perspectives, potentially causing them to miss out on opportunities for collaboration that could benefit their business. Elon Musk is certainly an independent thinker, but you could argue that, at times, his reactive behavior and impulsive thinking have resulted in a range of business problems and financial losses, legal and regulatory challenges, operational inefficiencies, and market volatility. These are unforced errors that have their roots in a lack of self-awareness.

A deficit of self-awareness turns a healthy bias for action into hasty decision-making that lacks thorough analysis or consideration of long-term consequences. When you opt for short-term gains over sustainable strategies, you get rushed product launches, poorly planned expansions, and reactive management.

These kinds of founders are cursed with a deficit of reflection. Without thinking things through slowly, they fail to learn from their mistakes or recognize their own repeating patterns of flawed reasoning. They're trapped in their own cognitive box. Their rigid thinking makes it challenging to acknowledge mistakes or adapt their thinking based on new information. Cognitive rigidity can also trap founders in a cycle of confirmation bias, where they only seek out information that supports their existing beliefs.

Self-Awareness and Toxic Behavior

In terms of behavior, many unsuccessful founders display a notable lack of discipline. They are addled with urgency. They don't plan and are perpetually in a hurry. They're loud, commanding and controlling, and generally unpleasant to be around. It usually takes a bucket of cold water in the form of some harsh 360 comments or stern feedback from a coach or investor for them to recognize these insidious patterns.

They micromanage and refuse to trust others with important tasks. This stifles autonomy and scares away creativity. It strains relationships. It's a huge millstone when it comes to building cohesive and motivated teams. Steve Jobs was known for his intense focus on the details at the expense of his coworkers' sanity.

All founders are workaholics, but their drive and dedication can result in neglecting personal well-being and work-life balance, leading to burnout and reduced effectiveness. Chronic stress can impair cognitive function, decision-making, and creativity, reducing their ability to lead effectively. It also sets a harmful precedent for the team, potentially leading to a toxic work culture. Marissa Mayer, the former CEO of Yahoo, was famous for her work ethic and long hours. But her inability to delegate effectively and tendency to take on too much personally led to criticism and a lack of sustained organizational change.

They are confrontational. Aggressive tendencies can create a hostile work environment, discouraging open communication and collaboration. Aggressiveness can lead to a fear-based workplace where employees are afraid to speak up or share ideas, stifling innovation and collaboration. Kalanick's aggressive and confrontational management style at Uber fostered a toxic workplace culture, contributing to numerous scandals and his eventual resignation.

They have huge behavioral blind spots. They can't recognize how their obnoxious behavior impacts their team and the company's morale. So, all the bad habits are left to fester, resulting in all kinds of unresolved conflicts, decreased employee engagement, and an overall toxic work environment that hampers the startup's progress. At the same time, they can't accept constructive criticism! Resistance to feedback often results in an echo chamber where only positive or agreeable input is acknowledged. So these founders suffer from a disease that is immune to diagnosis, and the same old mistakes keep happening.

Self-Awareness and Emotional Reactivity

Founders can be reactive, volatile, intimidating, and impulsive on their best days. When they're under particularly high amounts of stress, their lack of self-awareness results in even more unpleasantness. They can't recognize their own mental and physical fatigue. They keep trying to power through and ignore the signals from their body. They don't get enough sleep, and then it suddenly catches up with them. They might use drugs and alcohol to blunt the uncomfortable feelings and get through the week. Their insensitivity to their own feelings translates directly to group anxiety and burnout. They just keep pushing.

Founders generally have a heroic ability to handle stress, but everyone has a breaking point. Their tolerance can actually mask the symptoms of chronic stress until they become debilitating. Founders may push themselves and their teams too hard without realizing the brutal toll it takes. Sometimes there's a lot to be said for stepping back, counting to 10, and not sending the text.

Their aggressiveness and arrogance can contribute to quick tempers and impulsive reactions, making it difficult to manage emotions constructively. It often results in emotional outbursts that intimidate and alienate team members. This can create a culture of fear and resentment, reducing team cohesion and trust. Impulsive reactions driven by unchecked emotions can also lead to poor strategic decisions. Larry Ellison of Oracle is known for his aggressive and sometimes volatile behavior, which has led to numerous conflicts and lawsuits over the years.

How to Increase Self-Awareness

What are some concrete steps you can take to increase your own self-awareness?

Take time for reflection. If you prioritize slowing down and turning your attention inward, you may discover new ideas and insights. Even after a busy day or perhaps at the end of the week, think about recent events and actions, your feelings, and your learnings about what went right and what went wrong. Some questions to consider:

- Where did you feel great, inspired, in the zone, successful, and why?
- Where did you feel uncomfortable, discouraged, angry, or frustrated?
- Looking back, what would you do differently?
- What were your motivations behind your choices or behavior? Were you driven by fear, desire, curiosity, or something else?
- How did your emotions influence your behavior? Did you act out of anger, joy, sadness, or another emotion?
- Were there any old patterns popping up in your behavior?
- Was your behavior consistent with your values? Were there any discrepancies?
- How did your behaviors or decisions impact others?
- What do the reactions of others you impacted tell you about how they felt or viewed the situation? Were you oblivious, judgmental, or empathetic?
- What feedback did you receive from others? Did the feedback imply you have some blind spots and need to adjust your approach?
- Did any of your personal biases get in the way of being open to other views or alternatives? Did you let the facts win?

- What were the outcomes of your decisions? Were they what you expected? How can you learn from them?
- If things didn't turn out as you expected, how did you adapt?
- Which of your strengths and weaknesses impacted your responses to the situation?
- Did you miss any opportunities?
- Did you uncover any unforeseen problems?
- What insights have you gotten from the situation? Do these insights suggest that you must adapt or grow in any particular area?

Get feedback. Seek input from your team, investors, mentors, and partners. You can simply ask them about how they think a particular meeting went. Have your head of HR do it if you think people would be more open, or use an anonymous assessment or survey like a 360 to get quantitative ratings and comments. The trick is to avoid defensiveness or denial, be genuinely interested in the good and bad news, and use the process to identify areas for improvement.

Use a self-assessment tool. There are all kinds of these. They can be very helpful in giving you objective insights into your behavior and personality. Here are some of the more popular tools:

- Myers-Briggs Type Indicator (MBTI): The MBTI measures an individual's preferences across four dimensions (extraversion/introversion, sensing/intuition, thinking/feeling, and judging/perceiving) and assigns them to one of 16 personality types.
- DiSC assessment: DiSC is a behavior assessment tool that measures four personality traits: dominance, influence, steadiness, and conscientiousness. Understanding these traits can help leaders better understand their communication style and work more effectively with others.
- StrengthsFinder (CliftonStrengths): This assessment identifies an individual's top 34 strengths or talents. It encourages leaders to leverage their strengths in their work and personal lives.

- Emotional intelligence (EQ) tests: Several EQ tests are available, such as the Emotional Quotient Inventory (EQ-i) or the Mayer-Salovey-Caruso Emotional Intelligence Test (MSCEIT). These tests measure various aspects of emotional intelligence, such as self-awareness, self-management, social awareness, and relationship management.

- The Personality and Leadership Profile: This is Rich's program. It measures 46 personality traits, predicts 46 leadership, management, social skill, decision-making, and behavioral competencies using machine learning, generates the Hagberg Three Pillars of Leadership type, compares the individual to the "Best Leaders," and gives developmental advice.

- The Hogan Assessments: These personality assessments measure personality traits, values, and motives, focusing on how these characteristics can influence leadership performance.

- The Leadership Circle Profile: This 360-degree feedback tool evaluates a leader's effectiveness by gathering input from colleagues, subordinates, and supervisors. The assessment provides insights into the leader's strengths and areas for development.

- The Enneagram: This personality system assigns individuals to one of nine types based on their core motivations, fears, and desires. The Enneagram can help leaders better understand themselves and others, promoting better teamwork and communication.

- The Big Five personality test: The Big Five model measures five personality traits (openness, conscientiousness, extraversion, agreeableness, and emotional stability). By understanding these traits, leaders can gain insights into their behavior and decision-making processes.

Meditate. Meditation can calm the mind, increase mental focus, improve resilience and stress management, lower anxiety levels, improve sleep, increase creativity, reduce blood pressure, increase empathy, improve memory, strengthen the immune system, regulate mood swings, and improve general mental health and well-being. It increases self-awareness by fostering a greater sense of presence and focus on the present moment. It takes some discipline and cadence to start working properly, but it's well worth the effort. To quote David Lynch: "I thought when I started meditation that I was going to get real calm and peaceful, and it's going to be over. It's not that way; it's so energetic. That's where all the energy and creativity is."[3]

Get some coaching. There are a lot of great leadership coaches out there. This is an effective way to improve self-awareness, identify blind spots of personal performance and modify damaging patterns of behavior, identify areas where growth is needed, develop areas of strength and potential, learn to deal with challenging situations, and improve your ability to perform and get results. The process typically entails assessing strengths and weaknesses, setting developmental goals, learning about best practices and more effective ways of achieving these goals, and gaining a better understanding of yourself.

Above all, *stay curious*. Always look for opportunities for personal growth through reading, attending workshops, or participating in industry events. Be open to new experiences and willing to challenge your own assumptions and beliefs. Observe others—learn from other entrepreneurs by asking questions and seeing how they operate. Interrogate your own core values and principles. Try to figure out what makes you tick. Analyze your EQ, and improve your ability to recognize, understand, and manage your own emotions and those of others.

We are all works in progress.

PART III

Developing the Skills Required to Scale

A big part of Rich's work with founders involves deciding which areas to work on, which gaps to address. As we mentioned earlier in the book, Rich has spent decades identifying, documenting, and refining a list of 46 individual competencies that are highly correlated with effective leadership.

This is a daunting number. People can spend a lifetime working on half a dozen of these skills. If it takes that many skills to be an effective leader, how would an aspiring executive pick which ones to focus on?

That's where the 360 reviews come in. All of Rich's clients receive extensive 360 feedback from around a dozen or two key stakeholders (investors, board members, direct reports, and other key people), who are asked to rate the leader (on a five-point scale) on their *performance* for each of Hagberg's 46 competencies. But that's not all. Crucially, the stakeholders are also asked to rate how *important* each competency is to the success of the founder's job.

So how does Rich determine the areas to work on? By identifying the competencies with the biggest rating gaps between *performance* and *importance.* The differences in the data (the deltas) determine the competencies to address.

Before he began working with founders, Rich's experience told him that the strengths and gaps of general business leaders were all over the map. But with founders, it's a different story. Rich began to see the same patterns over and over again. Founders, Rich discovered, tend to share a surprisingly similar pattern of weaknesses. Delving into the personalities of founders, which we highlighted in parts one and two of this book, Rich began to understand what makes founders tick, and the ticking time bomb that is built into who they are. If you are a founder reading this book, chances are you need help with the following competencies. These are the areas that you're going to need to address if you want to defuse the time bomb:

- **Effective Decision-Making:** Founders are certainly decisive, but those decisions are often impulsive and poorly informed. Startups are rife with life-or-death decisions that depend upon sound judgment and reasoning, but founders tend to prioritize speed over deliberation. Their strong opinions and overconfidence can also intimidate employees, stifling the valuable input and collaboration needed to make a well-rounded decision.

- **Implementing Strategy:** Founders are often bad at implementing strategy. They constantly struggle to align their vision with concrete and actionable plans, leaving their hapless teams bereft of clear direction or realistic goals. Their fear of losing control (and resistance to input) results in disempowered employees, fragmented efforts, and a failure to adapt strategies to changing circumstances.

- **Planning, Prioritizing, and Maintaining Focus:** Founders are terrible at organized thinking. They are bombarded with competing needs and can easily fall prey to death by a thousand mental cuts. They get caught between their lofty vision and immediate crises, neglecting the tactical middle ground needed for operational clarity. Their tendency to chase opportunities without clear priorities (coupled with a fatal aversion to traditional planning processes) dilutes their resources and attacks alignment between teams.

- **Finding and Attracting Talent:** Too many founders ignore structured hiring processes and fail to prioritize recruiting. Their over-reliance on their own charm and vision also hinders their ability to engage candidates effectively, leading to mismatched hires that come back to haunt them.

- **Executive Team Building:** Founders are not natural team players. A company is only as committed and aligned as its executive team, but founders are frequently accustomed to being lone operators, hesitant to delegate authority or trust others to make decisions. This results in unclear roles and a lack of psychological safety, ultimately leading to all manner of dysfunction and inefficiency as the organization struggles to scale.

- **Delegation, Accountability, and Coaching:** These three competencies form a crucial triangle of execution, but founders are often dismal at delegation because they can't give up control, woeful at accountability because they can't clearly define the objectives, and incompetent at coaching because they're overly critical. They frequently find themselves in antagonistic relationships with the very people they need to realize their dreams.

- **Facilitating Conflict Resolution:** Founders often mishandle conflict by (a) picking sides, (b) imposing decisions without addressing the underlying issues, or (c) avoiding uncomfortable conversations altogether. As a result, the tensions fester, the trust erodes, and the team falls apart.

- **Developing Structures, Systems, and Processes:** You can't scale without them, but far too many founders dismiss these operational imperatives as bureaucracy. This misguided aversion creates all kinds of chaos as the company tries to scale, crippling sustainable growth and robbing teams of clear priorities and repeatable solutions.

Now, it's hard to blame founders for these gaps. These are all skills that executives in large organizations take decades to develop. Founders, unfortunately, have two distinct disadvantages: they don't have the time, and they lack the institutional knowledge of a mature organization. They have to learn all this material (a) very quickly and (b) in the midst of a five-alarm fire.

Tien distinctly remembers the session when Rich delivered (in excruciating detail) his "areas for improvement." His 10 weakest competencies were building teams, praise and recognition, delegation and empowerment, coaching, relationship building, culture management, holding people accountable, openness to input, finding and attracting talent, and planning, prioritizing, and maintaining focus. In other words, the classic "high IQ, low EQ" profile. It wasn't exactly a devastating medical diagnosis, but it sure felt like it. Rich basically held up an X-ray of Tien's leadership psyche and pointed out all the dark spots.

Tien spent a couple of weeks processing the news, poring over dozens of pages of scathingly honest 360 comments. Needless to say, there was plenty of soul-searching involved, not to mention plain old denial. But for every protest he could think of ("What do you mean I suck at planning and prioritization? I'm an engineer!"), Rich could point to his original personality profile and say, "Your personality test predicted all these 360 comments and ratings. This is who you are, Tien." Rich then synthesized the 360 feedback to create five distinct areas to work on:

- Building stronger teams and fostering collaboration
- Developing a culture of recognition and accountability
- Empowering and developing employees
- Strengthening communication and approachability
- Shaping a cohesive culture and vision

Tien had his marching orders. Thus began his decade-long journey with Rich to learn how to turn individual inspiration into collective execution.

The Good News: Natural Founder Strengths

Let's not forget the areas where founders typically excel. All these innate talents give you a great head start:

- **Creativity and Innovation:** Founding a startup often involves creating something new or offering a fresh perspective on an existing problem. Creativity fuels the problem-solving process and innovation helps the startup stand out in a crowded market.

- **Visionary Thinking:** Startups navigate uncertainty. Founders with visionary thinking can see the big picture, set long-term goals, and inspire the team to believe in the future of the company.

- **External Focus:** Successful startups understand their target market and the competitive landscape. External focus keeps founders attuned to customer needs and industry trends, allowing them to adapt their approach.

- **Adaptability:** The startup journey is filled with unexpected challenges and pivots. Founders who can adapt their strategies, embrace change, and learn from setbacks are better positioned to navigate the unknown.

- **Agent of Change:** Startups inherently disrupt the status quo. Founders who are agents of change can champion new ideas, motivate their team, and drive the company forward.

- **Inspirational Role Model:** Founders are often the heart and soul of a startup. Being an inspirational role model allows them to motivate and energize their team, fostering a culture of dedication and hard work.

- **Self-Confidence:** The startup world can be daunting. Founders with self-confidence can make tough decisions, persevere through setbacks, and convince investors and customers to believe in their vision.

- **Formal Presentation:** Founders need to effectively communicate their ideas to a variety of audiences, from investors to potential customers. Strong presentation skills allow them to clearly articulate their vision and win over stakeholders.

- **Taking Initiative:** Startups require a proactive approach. Founders who take initiative can identify problems, seize opportunities, and move the company forward without waiting to be told what to do.

- **Resilience and Stress Management:** The startup journey is stressful. Founders with resilience can bounce back from setbacks, manage pressure effectively, and keep moving forward even in challenging times.

Always remember: You're the entrepreneur, the founder, the person with the creative spark that can change the world. You see things that most people don't. The world needs you! Think of all the problems the world is facing now—the stakes could not be higher. But if you don't learn to get out of your own way, that spark won't have a chance to catch flame.

By all means, continue to hone your gifts. But if your stakeholders— investors, board members, advisors, direct reports, team members—are telling you in flashing red lights that you're struggling with a particular set of competencies, then it's time to pay close attention.

This isn't just a random list of generic advice for business executives. All of these competencies are data-driven and founder-specific, developed over years of working with startup leaders to help them connect the challenges they see in their own organizations with their own leadership weaknesses. Rich sees it time and time again: founders complaining about organizational issues that *exactly correlate* with their own competency gaps!

Notice how most of your positives as a founder relate to your talents as a solo performer, while the negatives generally relate to your role (or lack thereof) as a supportive team builder. In order to make it to the next level, you're going to have to use your talents to build a structure of focus, discipline, and organizational awareness.

After he spent a few weeks wandering in the woods with his 360 scores, Tien had a realization: *his stakeholders believed in him.* They weren't out to blindly trash him. They were completely invested in his success. They just needed him to learn some new skills (and learn them fast) in order for his company to make it to the next level.

So pull yourself together, and take a deep breath. We know which wires to cut. Now let's defuse that time bomb.

CHAPTER 9

Navigating the Rapids: Creating a Culture of Effective Decision-Making

R ich once worked with a founder who was the embodiment of brilliance and ambition. He had the vision to create a transformative financial services product, and the drive to push it forward. His decisiveness, charisma, and intellect inspired fear and admiration in equal measure. He was a force of nature that attracted talent, funding, press attention, and a healthy pipeline of intrigued prospects.

But then came a series of fateful decisions.

He picked the wrong target market to pursue. The founder was insistent: Fortune 500 or bust. The problem was that they were going after large, risk-averse enterprises that could never bring themselves to take a leap of faith and be the first to adopt an exciting new technology.

He overloaded the product. The features they built sounded amazing on paper but failed to address the more prosaic must-have needs of the user base. The product was essentially all exterior, no chassis.

He set the price too high. The assumption was that big companies pay big bucks. The result was a series of stunned and sticker-shocked meetings with prospect after prospect.

The result? The company went through four sales leadership changes in the span of two years, as someone always had to take the blame when sales did not materialize. In their last funding round, the company raised limited capital at a high valuation in order to minimize dilution, but they were running out of runway fast, and unable to find more funds without a damaging down round.

Now, was all this simply just the cruel, random fate of a typical startup, where sometimes you win, but most of the time you lose? Maybe. But as Rich told the founder, *every single one of these bad decisions could have been avoided*. All the market signals were there. All the customer feedback was there. All the in-house concerns were there. So what went wrong?

The founder, of course.

He was blinded by ego and made decisions based on pure gut instinct. In his previous company, for example, going for large companies was the right call, but this was a completely different product and market. So he fell prey to recency bias.

He didn't listen to his employees. He treated his job candidates and team members with a harsh, interrogative approach that sought to expose their "feet of clay" rather than inspire them. In a culture survey, one employee complained that he created an office atmosphere that recalled Stalinist Soviet Union.

He was equally dismissive of his customers. He belittled their intelligence, the sophistication of their industry, and their suggestions for improvement. One potential customer actually said, "He didn't want to listen; he just assumed we weren't smart enough to understand the value."

He didn't seek out new information. He was incurious. He didn't pay attention to the "sunflower" bias, where people tend to (a) agree with whatever the boss says and (b) only share good news, so he heard what he wanted to hear, versus the truth of what was actually happening.

After two years, his company only had one customer (and that one eventually quit). Put simply, the founder stubbornly drove the company off the cliff, convinced of his own infallibility. When it came to big, bet-the-company decision-making, his early assets—individual ego, drive, determination—quickly devolved into liabilities. Tick, tick, boom.

10 Questions: Effective Decision-Making

1. When faced with a high-stakes decision, do you prioritize speed over accuracy, hoping things will work out?
2. How often do you find yourself doubling down on decisions even when new evidence suggests you're on the wrong path?
3. Do you find it challenging to separate your instincts from impulsive reactions when making decisions under pressure?
4. Are you more likely to stick with a failing strategy because you've already invested too much to back out?
5. When making big decisions, do you tend to favor your own perspective over seeking input from others?
6. How frequently do you ignore early signs that a decision could have serious unintended consequences?
7. Do you focus more on maintaining control over decisions rather than empowering others to weigh in?
8. Are you prone to holding out for the "perfect" decision instead of moving forward with a workable one?
9. How comfortable are you with changing direction when data suggests that your initial choice wasn't ideal?
10. When a decision doesn't work out, do you tend to blame circumstances rather than assess your own approach?

How Bad Decisions Kill Startups

Consider the following list of decisions. As a founder, sooner or later you'll face every single one of them. None of these will be discrete events. You will be returning to these issues constantly throughout the lifetime of your startup. So, what binds them all together?

- Deciding on the product idea and the target market
- Deciding on who to partner with as a potential cofounder
- Deciding on a scalable business model

- Deciding when and who to hire to build a strong team
- Deciding what feedback to listen to when developing your product
- Deciding how to fund your startup's growth and which potential investors will bring the most value
- Deciding how to market your product to reach your target customers
- Deciding on which markets to enter or how to expand into new markets
- Deciding how and when to adapt your product, strategy, or business model
- Deciding on which strategic partnerships or alliances to pursue

Here's the answer: Mess up on just one of these, and you are sunk. You are done. These are what we call "bet the company" decisions. They are all potential extinction events. This helps explain why so many startups fail. It's a killing field out there. At any given moment, you can make a fatal decision without even realizing it. It also explains why it's imperative to build a general framework for effective decision-making.

Crucially, however, there is another dynamic at play regarding decision-making: velocity. Companies get slow (and ultimately become roadkill) when decisions are deferred. What's the sound of failure? A million cans kicked down the road. Here are some examples:

- **Feature overload:** An HR platform founder constantly changes their mind about core features, adding and removing elements based on fleeting trends instead of user data or a clear vision. The result? User confusion and anemic adoption.
- **Hiring hangover:** A founder constantly changes their mind about hiring more designers, developers, or marketers. This results in missed deadlines, communication gaps, and organizational exhaustion.
- **Market pivot paralysis:** A grocery delivery startup hesitates between focusing on store partnerships or building their own fleet, unsure which one to prioritize. In the meantime, competitors grab market share.

- **Funding fumble:** A fintech founder wavers between accepting a smaller, quicker investment to keep running or holding out for a larger, potentially game-changing deal. All this dithering drains resources, persecutes employees to the point of lunacy, and ultimately alienates both kinds of investors.

The ability to *expeditiously* combine knowledge with experience to make optimal decisions is at the heart of effective leadership, and all the more true for a founder-led startup. You create success or failure one decision at a time, and dozens of these turning points happen every single day. After all, your startup is simply the cumulative result of all your judgments thus far.

Bold, Decisive Leadership to Nowhere

Founders are strategically creative, exceptionally confident, and charmingly forceful. They act swiftly and decisively and are exceedingly comfortable with risk. Notice how none of this torrent of adverbs and adjectives suggests a propensity for sound, deliberate decision-making. In fact, it could indicate the exact opposite.

Founders are *forceful*. These people need to win, which means someone has to lose. They need to be right, which means that someone has to be wrong. When it comes to making tough decisions, founders often cross to a place where it's the fight that's most important, not the actual issue at hand. Their direct reports, however, tend to get tired of the gladiator treatment pretty quickly. In fact, they would just as soon avoid it altogether. So they fall back into "smile blankly and do what the boss says" mode. As a tragic result, the founder gets a false sense that their opinion is the right one, even when there's plenty of disconfirming data out there. They just haven't bothered to look.

They are *intuitive*. Their instinctive ability to make the right bet has brought them very far. They know their business better than anyone else (this happens to be true). So when it comes to making decisions, they go with their gut. But with growth comes complexity, often more than a single person can sufficiently absorb (including the founder). That's when their intuition breaks down. It's like giving an AI system flawed information: garbage in, garbage out. Founders rarely realize when they've passed this threshold, over-relying on their intuition for far too long.

They are *strategic*. They are big-picture thinkers. They see the forest, not the trees. When they make decisions, they go with what looks good from their perch high up in the intellectual stratosphere. They don't need to consider pesky specifics or details. Their eyes are set firmly on the horizon.

Founders aren't afraid of *risk*. They take on lots of it. That's who they are. But sooner or later, the dice are going to roll a different way, and if the risk is too great, then everything can come crashing down. But these founders don't consider the downside. They accelerate into the curve.

So what do all these attributes leave you with when it comes to making important decisions for a late-stage startup? One that is trying to navigate through all kinds of huge new complexities that require serious, organized initiatives? They leave you with the old way of doing things: solo heroism versus group collaboration, individual action versus collective analysis. Bold, decisive leadership to nowhere.

But wait, there's more.

Common Founder Mental Biases

As *Homo sapiens* with an elevated sense of self-worth, founders are particularly susceptible to a host of *mental biases*—or systematic patterns of deviation from rational judgment. The mind has all sorts of shortcuts for making decisions that are often expeditious and useful but are also capable of being wildly wrong. To quote Daniel Kahneman, who won a Nobel Prize on this topic: "Our comforting conviction that the world makes sense rests on a secure foundation: our almost unlimited ability to ignore our ignorance."[1]

So the bad news is that we, as humans, have a number of built-in biases that prevent us from making smart, objective decisions. That means founders, being members of the species (it's true—they're human), are already working from a shaky foundation. But here's the really bad news: their personality profiles, coupled with their corporate environments, make these biases *even worse*. Here are a few that they are particularly susceptible to:

- **Confirmation bias:** The tendency to interpret new evidence as confirmation of one's existing beliefs (while ignoring or discounting contrary evidence). Founders might selectively gather data or feedback that supports their vision while ignoring contradictory evidence. For example, a founder might continue to invest in a failing strategy because some data seems to support its potential, overlooking the overwhelming evidence that suggests otherwise.

- **Overconfidence bias:** Most founders strongly believe in their judgment and abilities, often more than is warranted. This overconfidence can lead to underestimating risks and overestimating the likelihood of success. A classic example is the assumption that their product will automatically succeed without extensive market research or user testing, resulting in product development that doesn't align with actual demand. To quote Kahneman again: "The confidence we experience as we make a judgment is not a reasoned evaluation of the probability that it is right."[2]

- **Survivorship bias:** This is the tendency to focus on the people or companies that "survived" while overlooking those that did not. Founders might model their strategies after successful companies, ignoring the *many more* that failed using similar approaches.

- **Anchoring bias:** This occurs when an individual relies too heavily on an initial piece of information (the "anchor") when making decisions. In the startup world, this could manifest as a founder fixating on a certain valuation or funding amount they want to achieve, influencing all subsequent negotiations and decision-making, potentially leading to unrealistic expectations or missed opportunities. One founder behavior that Rich sees constantly is anchoring around pedigree ("He worked at Google" or "She has an EE degree from MIT"), which often causes bad hiring decisions. Kahneman again: "People who have information about an individual case rarely feel the need to know the statistics of the class to which the case belongs."[3]

- **Sunk cost fallacy:** This is the tendency to continue a venture or project once an investment in money, effort, or time has been made, even if continuing is not the best course of action. A startup founder might continue pouring resources into a failing product because they've already invested heavily in it, rather than pivoting or cutting losses. Here's a prime example: sticking with a product idea or business model that worked in the beginning but now clearly isn't working any longer.

- **Bandwagon effect:** The tendency to do (or believe) things because many other people do (or believe) the same. In a startup context, this can lead to jumping on the latest trend or technology without fully analyzing if it's the right fit for their business. For example, investing in AI technology not because it's specifically beneficial to the business but because many VCs who invest in AI like to talk about it.

- **Fundamental attribution error:** The tendency to attribute mistakes that others make to their personality while blaming external factors for your own mistakes. For example: when someone is late to a meeting, it's their fault, but when *you're* late to a meeting, it's because of heavy traffic. Another example: a CEO blames the head of marketing for not creating a marketing strategy, but you can't set it effectively unless it supports a business strategy! Here's another one: blaming the sales team for lack of performance, when the founder isn't listening to customer complaints or keeping track of the competition. Salespeople can't sell flawed products.

- **Loss aversion:** The tendency to focus on the potential losses associated with a decision rather than the potential rewards. Look at what happened to IBM during the platform wars, or Yahoo during the search engine wars. You need to focus on the potential rewards of a decision, while also considering the potential risks.

To quote Kahneman again: "We can be blind to the obvious, and we are also blind to our blindness."[4]

What fresh hell is this? Founders don't even know the things they don't even know! They're blinded by both (a) dozens of mental biases and (b) a reverse-panopticon corporate environment that *completely exacerbates all of those mental biases*. They need to be right all the time, and they're being enabled by a group of smart executives who would much rather be nodding their heads and sharing good news than getting ripped to pieces during a heated discussion about a hard decision.

So what's the answer? How do founders get out of this mess, the mess in question being their own ego and bias-addled mind? How can they avoid their worst impulses in order to make effective, timely decisions?

Build a Decision-Making Machine

The most successful founders in our study have a framework for clarifying problems, considering multiple perspectives, weighing the facts, and evaluating the risk. This structured approach—where intuition complements rather than overrides analysis—ensures more sound and strategic decisions. In other words, these founders build themselves a decision-making machine.

Initiative is only worthwhile if it is informed by analysis. One of Rich's mentors once told him that he tended to treat a wisp of intuition like it was a four-lane highway of inspiration! He urged Rich *not* to ignore that spark but to treat it as one data point among many. In the *Harvard Business Review*, Sir Andrew Likierman summarizes his excellent research on the topic:

> I've found that leaders with good judgment tend to be good listeners and readers—able to hear what other people actually mean, and thus able to see patterns that others do not. They have a breadth of experiences and relationships that enable them to recognize parallels or analogies that others miss—and if they don't know something, they'll know someone who does and lean on that person's judgment. They can recognize their own emotions and biases and take them out of the equation. They're adept at expanding the array of choices under consideration. Finally, they remain

grounded in the real world: In making a choice, they also consider its implementation.[5]

In other words, your instinct for action needs to exist within a framework of deliberation.

Advice: How to Become an Effective Decision-Maker

Build a star chamber.

When it comes to decision-making, the biggest aha moment for lots of founders is that they no longer have to go it alone. You can *externalize* the decision-making that you used to do by yourself. Surround yourself with experienced voices, both inside and outside your startup. Focus on shifting from founder-centric decision-making to empowering capable team members. Find smart people with relevant domain experience and keep them in your circle. Above all, find people who will speak *plainly and honestly* with you—as Ali Ghodsi, the CEO of Databricks, told The Information: "As news travels up the chain, it becomes more and more positive, and by the time it reaches the very top, we don't have a problem anymore. It's just fantastic."[6] Get outside of the good news chain.

Take the time to carefully define the problem.

It's vitally important to define the problem clearly before jumping to possible solutions. When you gather the relevant facts, it might become clear that your original idea of what the problem was is just a symptom of another, larger problem. A founder's impatience can cause them to oversimplify a complex, multidimensional issue, especially if it has been persisting for a long time.

If you're not careful, you might wind up solving the wrong problem, building the wrong building, or curing the symptom rather than the disease. You have to ask the right questions and avoid jumping to conclusions. Take the time to understand the challenge, and use your team and advisors to help you see patterns in the facts.

Ask yourself: What would a successful outcome look like?
If you don't know where you're going, you'll end up someplace else.
—Yogi Berra[7]

Having a crystal-clear image of what you're trying to accomplish will also help you avoid making the wrong choice because you didn't clarify what was important. Start by identifying the ideal outcome of a given situation. Be specific about the qualities, benefits, and features of that outcome. Be realistic about what you can expect to get for your time and money.

For example, you might develop a long list of criteria for an ideal job candidate. What do you need the person to do and to accomplish? What is the most important knowledge, experience, and skill required to be successful? You might also be acutely aware that you are not likely to be able to find or afford that ideal job candidate, given your current stage of development or the attractiveness of your company's brand. So then you make some adjustments, but the important part is that you've identified what true north looks like.

Utilize a disciplined decision-making process.
Making decisions can be overwhelming, especially when there are many potential courses of action and a lot of unknown factors that could influence the outcome. If you follow a systematic process for decision-making, you can avoid costly mistakes. A structured framework should enhance your decision-making ability while reducing the impact of your own impulsiveness.

There are lots of models to choose from: Lean Startup methodology (or MVP), SWOT analysis (strengths, weaknesses, opportunities, and threats), decision matrices, decision trees, etc. However, they all share some fundamentals: a disciplined process of gathering information, identifying alternatives, weighing the pros and cons, and choosing the best course of action. Having a process in place can reduce the risk of making impulsive or emotional decisions.

Be flexible and open to new ideas.
**What the human being is best at doing is interpreting all new
information so that their prior conclusions remain intact.**
—Warren Buffett[8]

As a founder, holding on to your innate sense of curiosity is foundational to making smart decisions. Founders need outside input. Because it is easy for them to hold tightly to their original idea or opinion and be influenced by unconscious biases, consulting with team members, mentors, and advisors is very useful. Never underestimate your capacity to rationalize anything you want to do—or your constant need to be right.

If you listen and seek feedback and constructive criticism, it will help you identify potential problems and opportunities for improving your decision-making. It can help you identify alternatives, facts, and views you may not have considered. Good decisions come from a broad base of facts, generating multiple alternatives and an openness to input. Your stubbornness can be your downfall.

Learn the difference between intuition and impulse.
Both intuition and simple impulsiveness involve the sense that you know something without engaging in deliberate analysis. Both create a sense of urgency to act quickly on an insight. Both can be powerful motivators to act. But there's a difference between the two. Intuition originates from experience and knowledge and involves the subconscious processing of all facts and patterns you have accumulated throughout the course of your career. Impulse is driven by emotion that gets triggered by fear, excitement, or anger. Intuition is more calm and grounded. Impulse is frantic and reactive.

The stress and pressure of a startup can overwhelm a founder and make it difficult to differentiate between intuition and impulse. Their ego may cause them to misinterpret their confidence or simple desire as intuitive insights. If leaders aren't attuned to their emotional state, they might mistake emotional reactions for intuitive insights.

Use your impulse to trigger your intuition. Slow down and reflect. Ask yourself where your motivation to act is *really* coming from. Get input from others with different viewpoints. This is where emotional intelligence enhances your ability to interpret that feedback as well as secure buy-in to your decisions. Gather research, face the hard facts, and objectively assess the pros and cons of your insight. While data and input from others are critical, don't discount your intuition. As a founder, you likely have a good sense of what's best for your business. Trusting your gut can be a valuable tool when making difficult decisions, especially when you've done your due diligence and have weighed the pros and cons. It simply makes things move faster.

Consider the risks. Ask disconfirming questions.

When Reid Hoffman came up with the idea for LinkedIn, he recounted at a Greylock event, "I went around to all of my smart friends and asked, 'What's wrong with this idea? Why won't this work?'"[9] Founders are often overconfident and overly optimistic. Most of the "bet the company" decisions and even many day-to-day decisions involve some uncertainty and some risk.

Whenever Rich hears the phrase "It's high risk, but it's high reward" from a founder, his alarm bells start ringing. It's important to consider exactly *what* might go wrong and what are the potential risks that might impact the alternatives you are considering. Because it is easy for leaders to exert undue influence on their team with their strong opinions, it is important to ask *disconfirming questions*: What could go wrong? What have I not considered? What could make my proposed solution fail? Do I have any assumptions that should be challenged?

■ ■ ■

To sum up, effective decision-making isn't a mystical talent. It's a skill crafted over time, blending analytical thinking with empathy, risk management, resilience, and intellectual humility. Smart founders don't rest on their innate abilities; they grow through disciplined reflection, calculated risk-taking, and a willingness to learn. By balancing data with insight, courage with caution, and strength with adaptability, they build decision-making practices that create lasting value and inspire those around them.

CHAPTER 10

From Dictator to Facilitator: How to Implement Strategy

A wildly popular e-commerce company appears to have it all: a huge social media following, hundreds of millions in funding, and a charismatic founder. But rapid growth brings rapid problems: legacy systems, legal challenges, massive burn rates, and new competition. Unfortunately, the founder seems more concerned with managing his status as a social media celebrity than managing all these new enterprise-level issues.

Here's what the founder thinks: He created a successful company (and disrupted an entire industry in the process) because of his vision, creativity, and willingness to *act*. It's not like he's slacking—he rigorously pursues what inspires him and promotes his company night and day. He can always hire for execution.

"He had this great personal story—he started this amazing company from nothing," says one anonymous 360 commenter. "But now that we've hit some bumps in the road, he's clearly not as interested in managing the day-to-day. Between his story and his company, he chose his story."

The board makes him hire an old-school disciplinarian COO, but the founder resists him at every turn. As a result, there's no alignment. There's no broader strategic plan. The company pivots and pivots, wasting its resources and demoralizing its employees, and eventually files for bankruptcy.

What Is Strategy?

Here's a popular image of how strategy works: A founder retreats to their corner office, surveys the market, sizes up the competition, assesses the product road map, weighs the resources at hand, and then delivers the annual master plan to the organization.

Which is, of course, complete nonsense.

Strategy is not some tablet set in stone. Strategy is *alignment*. It is an ongoing, dynamic process. Picture a big rubber band that wraps around all the elements of your startup. That rubber band is your strategy. Eric Van den Steen once memorably described it as "the smallest set of choices to guide other choices."[1]

Strategy is flexible, adjusting its shape while maintaining its core purpose. It provides a broad alignment that links objectives to actions while providing flexibility in achieving goals. It is not some grand edict but rather an evolution of a central value proposition through continually changing circumstances.

10 Questions: How to Implement Strategy

1. Do you have a clear strategy that your entire team understands and aligns with, or is your organization moving in multiple directions?
2. How often do you set ambitious goals without breaking them down into actionable steps and realistic timelines?
3. Do you prioritize your company's long-term vision over short-term gains, or do immediate pressures often derail strategic planning?
4. Are you actively involving your team in strategic planning, or do you rely on a top-down approach that leaves them out of the loop?
5. When plans are in motion, do you regularly check progress and adjust based on results, or do you stick to the original plan regardless of changing circumstances?

6. How frequently do you assess and update your understanding of customer needs to ensure your product remains aligned with market demands?

7. Is your strategic vision supported by the necessary operational systems and processes, or are you just hoping things will fall into place?

8. Do you regularly evaluate the risks associated with your strategic initiatives, or do you focus solely on potential rewards?

9. Are your team members clear on how their roles contribute to the broader strategy, or do they struggle to see the connection between their tasks and the company's goals?

10. How effectively do you balance innovation with strategic focus, ensuring that new ideas enhance your long-term vision rather than distract from it?

Fear and Loathing: Why Founders Struggle with Strategy

Many founders struggle with the concept of strategy for a simple reason—they've gotten along fine without it so far. Their bright idea has resulted in funding, employees, and an actual product with actual customers. To them, strategy is all business school theory, where the rubber meets the sky.

But sooner or later, everything will start to fall apart. The old way of doing things will simply not work anymore. Your strengths as a founder—a headstrong vision, a bias for action—will suddenly turn problematic. What shot you into space isn't going to get you to Mars.

When we look at Rich's data comparing the personalities and behaviors of highly strategic founders to their less successful peers, some clear patterns emerge. When we map the personality data of nonstrategic founders (the way they see themselves) to their corresponding 360 data (the way others see them behave), a very dark cloud appears on the horizon.

Low-strategy founders are driven by fear and anxiety. Strategy is about looking into and trying to predict the future and then adjusting your plan. All founders must deal with huge levels of stress, uncertainty, critical decisions, multiple options, endless problems, and awareness that their lack of experience and knowledge is making it increasingly difficult to feel comfortable in their role as captain of the ship. So, it's not surprising that unsuccessful founders tend to obsess about the future and what could go wrong.

On top of that, they don't have a plan that they feel confident about. They are constantly afraid of failing. They admit that they are tense and emotional. They are plagued by crippling doubts. Their insecurity makes them easily hurt by criticism, so they don't benefit from feedback. They are stressed and distracted and admit having difficulty concentrating (their colleagues concur).

These people are pessimistic about the world in general. They operate from a dark place of unease and urgency. Needless to say, it's hard to make good strategic decisions and provide clear, consistent direction when your inner life is so chaotic. They're deeply insecure but try to project confidence, which often comes across as arrogance. Outwardly, they are aggressive, impatient, and reactive. We've known these kinds of people all our lives. Several public figures come to mind.

But what does all this insecurity, fear, and anxiety have to do with strategy? A lot, as it turns out.

They don't benefit from the wisdom of teams. These founders live in a zero-sum world. They tend to regard other people as competitive threats, if they regard them at all. So they're incapable of benefiting from the broad array of perspectives that you need to generate an effective strategy and equally dismal at gathering the collective buy-in you need to execute it: "I'm pretty sure that in his heart, he didn't value (a) the input of his team and (b) the value of planning. So we began to wonder if he knew where he was taking the company."

They mistake tactical activity for strategic productivity. They work all the time, but they don't get much done. They start things, but they don't finish them. As a result, plans never get off the ground. Strategic initiatives are just new opportunities to fail. They leave behind a trail of heavily scribbled whiteboards and not much else: "Lots of ideas, but very little in the way of execution, which is scary. Right now, it feels like we are AOL in the dial-up era of the internet. If we don't pivot fast, we are hosed."

When they do set strategic goals, those goals are often wildly unrealistic. They underestimate risks and challenges. They constantly disregard downsides and costs. They don't do their research. They don't listen to dissenting points of view. They neglect real threats and miss out on potential opportunities. Needless to say, this is very dangerous when you're putting together a reality-based strategic plan! The result is management by crisis: "He rules by fiat and keeps the product road map very close to his chest, so we have no idea how to respond to new competition, new market dynamics, new anything. He keeps telling us that we have the best product. That we're smart, and we can figure it out."

They can't adapt their strategy (if they have one at all). Insecure founders feel they have to make all the strategic decisions because they can't rely on people. All that fear spawns distrust. As a result, they get incredibly defensive when things don't pan out. They stick to their guns: "We seem to be stuck in place—there are no plans that go beyond the next quarter, no meaningful road map or any documented long-term plan."

Ultimately, they can't translate their vision into actionable strategy. They are headstrong and persuasive and can convince anyone over a cup of coffee that they are about to change the world. But they can't turn all those grand ideas into concrete plans: "He seems to enjoy going through the motions of thinking strategically, but his vision seems to be disconnected from reality. The vision also seems to change from quarter to quarter, which tends to hinder his credibility."

You may recognize some of these traits in yourself. After all, fear and anxiety go with the job. Stress is the water you swim in. This is an industry with a 90% failure rate. But here's the good news: Most strategic founders started as nonstrategic founders. In addition to putting in the hard work of identifying and addressing their worst impulses, they also figured out that strategy is ultimately about finding *alignment*, not finding a series of answers to a series of problems.

Strategic CEOs don't exist on some separate plane from aggressive early-stage founders. They are *former* aggressive early-stage founders. The vision is still there; it's just that they've channeled it into a strategy that takes advantage of the wisdom of teams. They've figured out that their auto-pilot tendencies will only take them so far. So they've adapted. They've dialed down the transactionality and the distractions and leaned into team-work and strategic vision. They face reality and the facts and make decisions based on objective input rather than being hijacked by their ego and fears.

What Goes Wrong Without Strategy

When you're just starting, the scientific method constitutes your strategy. When all you have is a series of educated guesses, you simply test them and adjust your ideas according to the results: build, measure, learn, repeat. Building a minimum viable product (and trying to find customers who aren't family members) will get the ball rolling on broader "strategic" issues: competitive dynamics, resource allocation, and unit economics. At this stage, strategy is what comes from tactics.

But watch out. You still have to build strategy. The seed stage involves chasing anything that moves, but this behavior can get you into big trouble in the traction stage. It's one of the top reasons companies stall out. You will need organizational alignment to address new challenges like formal-izing your culture, expanding into new regions and markets, designing the organization, or building competitive moats. Without a central framework guiding all these decisions, you're going to waste a lot of effort and money dealing with pissing contests and ego parades.

It's a mistake, for example, to conflate a product road map with a strategy. The latter is much broader. Your product sits inside that rubber band, along with all sorts of elements: a culture plan, a hiring plan, a financial plan, a competitive plan, and a growth plan. You still want orga-nizational focus. You still want cultural "fit." Neglect any one of these elements and you're in trouble. Approach any of them as isolated issues, and you're dead.

Strategic founders understand this balance and use strategy to *enable* (not inhibit) creativity and growth. They often excel in ideation and leader-ship but desperately need help with the operational efficiency part. Strategy forces them to confront those weaknesses, but the good news is that they don't have to do it alone. It's a collaborative process, not a pep talk at a leadership meeting.

Here's what could go wrong if you neglect strategy:

- **Operational scaling:** At some point, you need to develop systems, processes, and infrastructure to handle the increases in production, customer service, and team size. Everyone tells you this can be done without compromising quality or speed, but you're deeply suspicious of these claims. And guess what? You're right! There are always delays and problems when you invest in new infrastructure. But you don't realize that to eventually speed up, you have to slow down first. So you stick with what works, duct-taping over the problem areas while the ship slowly sinks into the ocean.

- **Advanced financial management:** Your CFO is telling you that you need to step up your game in more sophisticated financial planning and management, including detailed forecasting, revenue optimization, and possibly preparing for an IPO or acquisition. You might think that projecting out your company's finances over one year, let alone three, is patently ludicrous. But you're missing the point: You need to learn these new behaviors because they will eventually bring new insights. Even if it feels purely tactile and process-oriented at first, you need to go through these motions to genuinely understand the fiscal health of your company.

- **Building a brand:** Your CMO is telling you that you need to start thinking about long-term brand building, establishing a market position, and creating a loyal customer base through customer experience strategies. As someone with an innate aversion to bullshit, when you hear terms like "corporate branding," you immediately think of consultants and money and endless meetings. But this is simply the next layer of atmosphere on your climb up the mountain, and you need to acclimatize. Otherwise, you'll stay stuck in a product mindset and set yourself up for commodification. You'll become a software feature that a bored Microsoft engineer will idly decide to co-opt one night.

- **Talent acquisition and development:** You understand you need to invest in recruiting top talent, developing leadership, and cultivating a culture that can sustain rapid growth and change. This all sounds fine in theory. But you know that building a team isn't like going grocery shopping. You're hiring for job descriptions that don't even exist yet. What's wrong with hiring smart, motivated people who will learn on the job? Nothing, but there are areas of expertise you *simply don't have* as a traction-stage company that you will need to reach the next level. And if you don't have some kind of leadership development structure in place, then people will get bored, or alienated, or disincentivized . . . and they will punch out.

Here is the basic founder objection against leaping into corporate strategy too early: Startups are not smaller versions of larger companies. Big companies know their markets, their customers, and their business model. Startups are still trying to figure out how to make money! Sure, strategy is important, but if we don't stay flexible and iterative, we won't have a foundation to build on.

It's a valid complaint. That's why strategic planning for startups should emphasize an iterative and incremental method of formalizing your business model. Flexibility and modification based on experience and feedback shape the plan, which is constantly revised and revisited. Nothing stays static for long.

Why? Because your new reality in the traction stage demands these shifts. Eventually, the priorities will shift: from finding product-market fit to scaling operations, from being efficient with limited resources to optimizing them for expansion and competition, from life-or-death bets to calculated risks, from quick solitary decisions to deliberate processes with multiple stakeholders, from a loose "undergraduate" culture to a structured set of values. You need to switch from being an opportunistic individualist to a deliberate facilitator.

Everything becomes more complex: operations, market dynamics, resource management. Stakeholders expect more stability and predictability. You'll face a whole new raft of competitors, requiring a shift in how you position yourself. You need to create a burning platform that drives change. You need to deliver "WTF"-level product features that aren't merely compelling but fundamentally transform your customer experience. And you can't solve problems simply by throwing people at them anymore.

The old ways must be unlearned.

The Perennial Questions

Some strategic questions simply won't go away. They will never be fully answered. They assume different dimensions at different stages of growth, but their premises remain the same. People at the top of huge enterprise companies wrestle with these questions. Founders with a few colleagues and some seed funding wrestle with these questions. They are perennially relevant in good times and bad.

- *Are we aligned with our mission and values?*
  Is this who we are? Make sure that your company's growth and strategic decisions stay true to its core mission and values. It's essential for maintaining a cohesive culture and brand integrity.
- *Do we deeply understand our customers' evolving needs?*
  If you lose the customer, you lose the company. Given the dynamic nature of markets, it's vital to keep a pulse on customers' changing problems, preferences, and perceptions. This helps refine product offerings and customer experiences.
- *Are our products and services still solving the right problems?*
  Product-market fit is never done. You need to constantly reassess the market fit of your product, encouraging innovation and adaptation in response to market shifts or technological advancements.
- *What emerging trends or technologies could impact our industry or business?*

What's coming around the corner? Anticipating and reacting to industry trends and technological advancements can give you a competitive edge, whether adopting new technologies or pivoting business models.

- *How can we improve our operational efficiency and scalability?*
  There will always be things to improve. Continuously seeking ways to enhance operations and scalability is crucial for sustainable growth. This includes evaluating systems, processes, and team structures.

- *Are we effectively balancing short-term needs with our long-term vision?*
  To quote Peter Drucker: "Long-range planning does not deal with future decisions, but the future of present decisions."[2] You need to make sure that your immediate decisions and actions contribute to the long-term strategic objectives rather than just addressing short-term pressures.

- *How can we foster more innovation and creative thinking within the team?*
  How do we build the machine that builds machines? Encouraging a culture that values creativity and innovation supports problem-solving and can lead to breakthrough products or solutions.

- *Are we making data-driven decisions?*
  Let the facts win. Instilling a culture of measuring, analyzing, and acting on data helps ensure that your decisions are grounded in reality rather than intuition alone.

- *How can we improve team dynamics and communication?*
  There needs to be open dialogue about strategic decisions and how to execute the strategy. For starters, you need to hear the views of team members who have relevant domain expertise. This helps to create buy-in, which is crucial to developing a sound strategic plan and ultimately executing that plan.

- *What are our competitors doing better, and what can we learn from them?*

Turn your competitors into your teachers. Understanding their product strengths and weaknesses, competitive positioning, and strategies can reveal gaps in your own strategy and provide opportunities for differentiation. How does their product compare with yours? How are they positioning themselves in the market? What customers are they targeting? What's their pricing model? What's their go-to-market strategy (self-service, enterprise, etc.)? Are they innovating? Are they financially sound? Are they facing any legal challenges?

- *Are we effectively managing risk and preparing for potential setbacks?* Is there a Plan B? Considering potential risks and having contingency plans will help you navigate through tough times without derailing your mission.

The famous Peter Drucker line is that "culture eats strategy for breakfast." But that assumes that culture and strategy are mutually exclusive. That's simply not true. Each informs the other. Adjusting your strategy as your startup grows is crucial for staying relevant, competitive, and culturally aligned. It's about adapting to new realities, optimizing for larger operations, and continuously aligning the company's objectives with market needs and internal capabilities. This evolution separates enduring businesses from those that fade away after some bright and sparkly initial success.

Advice: How to Implement Strategy

Fire yourself early.
It's a mistake to think that strategy only comes from the top. That it can only be delivered by a chosen founder bearing the holy tablets. In the early stages, maybe that's accurate, but eventually, the Peter Principle takes hold. As your organization grows, the complexity multiplies exponentially. There are just too many pieces. If you're not already incompetent in certain aspects of your business, that incompetence will be thrust upon you.

The good news is that *Homo sapiens* are capable of cooperating in large numbers. The bad news is that to make that happen, you have to give up control. And that's hard for founders. Usually, one of two things happens. They disempower their managers, continue to dictate marching orders, and precipitate all sorts of resentment. Or they completely check out and assume a "zen-like" hands-off approach, and everything goes off the rails. It all ends badly. In both cases, they're sending chaos downstream. Ambiguity reigns. You need to get out of a top-down broadcast mode and become more of a listener and a synthesizer.

That's when you go to your team and say: "You guys know the problem. You are closest to the seam. I might have ideas, but your hands are on the steering wheel. I am simply not able to keep my hands around all the dynamics that are happening in the marketplace, the sentiments we're getting from customers, the challenges we're dealing with in product development, the everyday operational issues. Now, I can try to learn as much as possible and employ the David Packard approach of MBWA (Management by Walking Around),[3] but ultimately, no one will figure this out better than you."

It's important to push hard problems down the structure when developing a strategic plan. That way you get better decisions, and you get better buy-in. Remember, truly strategic thinkers are relatively rare. You need to find the people who are truly capable of strategic thinking: connecting the dots, seeing things dispassionately, overcoming biases, and surfacing the most important issues. Why? Because those people know where the actual answers live.

Make strategic planning a habit, not an event.

A strategic plan should answer three key questions: Where are we? Where do we want to go? How will we get there? It's not something that gets magically generated at a budget off-site. Strategy development is a continual process. Lengthy and deliberate strategic planning processes aren't just for big companies. Don't think that one big meeting will handle it. The idea is to avoid discrete rectilinear thinking toward a recurring, iterative approach. Make strategy a habit, not an event.

Here's one model: Conduct the research in the first half of the year. What's the biggest obstacle in our way? There's always one that's bigger than the others. Talk to the customers, the employees, the investors. Find out what you need to do to succeed next year. Then, spend the summer pitching ideas, and use a fall board meeting as a forcing function to present your plan for the next fiscal year. Then, after some more tinkering, you present the plan to the company at the sales kickoff meeting at the beginning of the year.

That strategic plan drives the go-to-market. It drives the budget. It informs the organizational chart. And it arrives, of course, around the same time that you start doing the listening for the next strategic planning process. Think in terms of cycles, not single points in time. Schedule quarterly reviews to assess your progress toward these objectives, reevaluate your strategies, and make adjustments in your plan as needed as things change. This ensures your day-to-day operations align with your long-term goals. In this story, no one finds product-market fit and lives happily ever after.

Apply the "green, yellow, red" implementation framework.
How do you know when your strategy is working? When your employees wake up in the morning knowing (a) why they are working for your company, (b) what the corporate strategy is, and (c) how they can contribute to that strategy by achieving specific goals and objectives. That's the ideal green light situation.

A yellow light situation contains a gap. One of those three elements—why, what, how—is missing. It's usually the last one. Yes, you can see the broader argument for the company. Yes, you have the OKRs (objectives and key results) or the milestones to hit. No, you have no idea how to hit those objectives. But at least that discussion starts with both sides agreeing on the basic argument. Then, it's a question of iterating, experimenting, and figuring out a problem together. That's the benefit of a solid strategy—it's not just two people arguing against themselves. There's a third object in the room.

A red light is a three-item strikeout. The person isn't engaging in any argument, broader plan, or specific action item. They're unhappy. They're disgruntled. They're complaining about the cereals in the break room. Hopefully, this is a rare situation, and the person can either make a conscious decision to engage or they can move on. But what if it's not that rare? What if it describes the general sentiment of the organization as a whole?

Yikes. In that case, you probably don't even have a why, much less a what. In which case, you can forget about the how.

Establish a three-year road map.
Three years is a Goldilocks amount of time—not too short, not too long. Afterward, break your three-year road map into yearly priorities, clearly laying out the milestones and short-term goals that operationalize the long-term plan. What are the most important things that your company needs to achieve each year? What do you want to achieve by the end of each year? These outcomes should be specific, measurable, achievable, relevant, and time-bound (SMART).

Review your road map regularly. As your company grows and changes, it may need to be updated. Communicate your road map to your team. Make sure that everyone understands your vision, priorities, and goals. This will help everyone stay motivated and focused on achieving their tasks at hand. Ask each functional or group leader to communicate to their team or function how their goals fit into the overall plan.

Be realistic about your goal setting.
Goals should stretch your startup, but they also need to be achievable. At Google, for example, achieving 70% of your OKR qualifies as success, while completely accomplishing it is considered an extraordinary performance.[4] Define what success looks like for each goal, break them down into actionable steps, and share these with your team. Founders need to articulate clear, quantifiable objectives that are challenging yet attainable.

Then, they need to break these larger goals into smaller, actionable tasks while communicating expectations and timelines to each team member to ensure everyone is aligned.

Make data-driven decisions when setting goals. If you aim to increase sales by 20%, for example, consider your current sales growth rate and the actions you'll need to take to achieve that increase. This will help ensure your goals are grounded in reality.

A founder must know the team's abilities, skills, and capacity for work. Many early-stage startup teams are made up of people learning their roles on the job (this often includes the founder). Setting goals that are *just beyond* the current skill level can promote growth and improvement without becoming overwhelming.

Finally, goals should not be set in stone. Review them regularly and adjust if necessary. If the business climate changes or your team's capacity changes, your goals should adapt, too. Celebrating small victories along the way helps to keep morale high and demonstrates progress toward the larger objective. This encourages the team to continue pushing for the bigger objective.

Embrace a structured planning process.

Successful goal setting often involves disciplined planning methods, such as the OKR framework, which focuses on setting ambitious objectives and measurable key results.[5] These OKRs should cascade down through the entire organization, with each level aligning its objectives to higher-level goals.

Take advantage of the iterative Agile methodology, dividing larger tasks into smaller, manageable sprints, making the process more flexible and adaptable and ensuring everyone on the team understands their role in achieving the overall objectives.[6] Also, consider adopting planning techniques like SMART goals. This framework helps create clear, attainable objectives and is a good example of a traditional business practice that can benefit startups.

Founders often paint a high-level picture of what is in their heads but don't translate that lofty vision into more concrete goals, outcomes, deliverables, metrics, or milestones. What does success look like on a monthly, quarterly, and annual basis?

■ ■ ■

To sum up, strategy *isn't a static directive*. It's a flexible framework for aligning objectives with actions amid evolving circumstances. It's a living, dynamic process, essential not just for navigating current challenges but for sustaining growth and alignment in the long term. And it can't be dictated from on high. When you make the leap from dictator to facilitator, you inspire a culture of accountability, innovation, and clarity. By engaging your teams, setting realistic but ambitious goals, and continually revisiting your approach, you can cultivate an organization that thrives in complexity and remains focused on its mission.

CHAPTER 11

The Bridge Between Strategy and Execution: Planning, Prioritizing, and Maintaining Focus

> If I know how you spend your time, then I know what might become of you.
>
> —attributed to Goethe

In the mid-nineties, Rich had a thriving professional services firm that mostly did leadership coaching, a business he had done for 15 years and knew well. So, to expand his services in an effort to grow, he launched a new effort to help companies assess and change their organizational cultures.

He started by getting 24 of Silicon Valley's biggest companies to complete his beta version free of charge, and this effort landed his first paying client, Hewlett-Packard. He got a call from Lew Platt, the CEO, who surprised him by saying that he wanted to have Rich "help me change the culture of the Hewlett-Packard Company." This catapulted his firm into a new line of business.

But these culture change efforts turned out to be incredibly complex projects that tested the systems and processes of his firm. They could involve tens of thousands of respondents and big, complex projects. Then came the asteroid that almost took out the entire company.

Soon after the HP project, two huge banks reached out for help when they were planning to merge and wanted to understand the differences between their cultures in an effort to make the integration smoother. Over 60,000 employees filled out Rich's survey. The scale of the project almost broke the firm. It was difficult, painstaking work involving dozens of different departments within each given company—like running 15 to 20 projects at the same time.

It was all too much: too many respondents, too many business units and functions, too much data, too much volume straining the systems. The systems (such as they were) were completely overloaded. The logistics were spiraling out of control.

Rich realized something needed to change. At the same time that his firm had more work than ever, *each project was taking more time to complete.* His company needed to track time and manage costs or end up losing money on the project. They needed project management on a level that they had never done before. This resulted in a lot of stress, a lot of work hours, a lot of in-house arguments, and a lot of confusion about who did what. They simply had to do better at execution, and Rich was starting to think that he was part of the problem.

Rich decided to take his own medicine. The change needed to start from the top. He asked his employees for a thorough 360 review of his performance as CEO. In other words, "Physician, heal thyself." He got absolutely abysmal scores on all of the measures of execution, and his number-one competency gap was focus and prioritization. Here are some direct quotes:

- "Rich can be a lot of fun to work with, but project management and maintaining focus are not his strengths."
- "It can be unclear which activities or projects are the most important."
- "He's not big on goal setting or clarifying responsibilities."
- "He's a P (Perceiving) on the Myers-Briggs! What do you expect?!"

- "He's great with ideas and research, but for everything else, gosh, don't get me started."

And so began a long, slow journey of trying to get organized, both personally and professionally, in the midst of a maelstrom. A big part of that effort involved promoting his colleague Stacy McKinney to COO (10 years later, she would be running the healthcare strategy practice of a huge consulting firm). It also entailed Rich learning three important things: how to plan to achieve his strategic objectives, how to relentlessly prioritize in order to keep that plan going, and how *not* to get distracted by anything else.

10 Questions: Focus, Prioritizing, and Planning

1. Do you have a clear sense of your company's most pressing priority, or are you overwhelmed by an endless list of urgent tasks?
2. Are you devoting your time to high-impact activities that drive growth, or are you frequently sidetracked by minor tasks and distractions?
3. How effectively do you distinguish between urgent tasks and those that are truly important for your company's future?
4. When facing numerous tasks, do you prioritize based on their impact, or do you try to tackle everything at once?
5. How often do you find yourself firefighting, reacting to immediate issues rather than working toward long-term goals?
6. Do you feel that your day-to-day activities align with your strategic vision, or are you constantly shifting focus?
7. Are you actively eliminating distractions, or do emails, messages, and meetings routinely break your concentration?
8. How disciplined are you about following through on plans, ensuring that projects reach completion rather than losing momentum?
9. Do you delegate effectively, or are you handling tasks that could be managed by others to keep your focus on critical priorities?
10. Are you regularly reviewing and adjusting your objectives based on progress, or do you set goals without much follow-up?

The Challenge for Founders

What's the difference between a strategist and a planner? Strategy is about lifting your gaze from the map to the horizon and envisioning where you want your startup to be months, years, or even decades down the line. But you're not just setting a final destination—you're also thinking about the different pathways you can take to get there, anticipating possible challenges and preparing for them. This entails creating a *dynamic* strategic planning process that continually adapts to the changing business landscape. It also means communicating this long-term vision to your team in such a way that they understand their role in achieving it, fostering a legitimate sense of purpose and direction.

Planning is a different beast. It's about what to do, here and now. It's about focusing on immediate goals, defining what each team member needs to do, setting targets, and assigning responsibilities. It's the groundwork that ensures your startup keeps running smoothly day by day. Think of it as plotting the steps on a hike to make sure you can reach the next checkpoint without getting lost. It's crucial for keeping the team aligned and making sure everyone knows what they need to work on.

According to their team members, the few founders who actually rate high on planning are generally perceived to be more dependable and decisive. Unlike their peers, they are not distracted by unimportant details. They know the importance of establishing short-term goals, clarifying roles and responsibilities, and setting priorities and milestones. They are the builders: frameworks, systems, processes. They share information. They also hold people accountable.

According to their personality tests, this rare breed of founders is generally more deliberate and consistent in their thinking. They don't get carried away by their feelings. They like things to be under control. They are clear thinkers who are more likely to stick with familiar things and more focused on getting it right before they act. They are "measure twice, cut once" people. But that also means they are less inclined to take risks or come up with novel hacks or workarounds.

The point, however, is not to shift from being a strategist to being a planner. The point is to be aware of your weaknesses and hire accordingly. Most founders still haven't learned that structure can actually *amplify* creativity by giving it space and discipline.

Founders tend to fly 30,000 feet in the sky—or three feet off the ground. They are either contemplating the universe or reacting to an immediate crisis. Notice how neither scenario involves delivering implementation plans with well-defined strategic objectives, short-term goals, and clear priorities. In the mind of the founder, there's no tactical middle altitude between the universal and the local. They can't translate their vision into a clear set of strategic objectives, nor can they clarify short-term priorities and goals to give the organization immediate direction. So, they scatter their efforts.

They may not realize it, but they are creating an adversarial relationship with their own organization. Even though *they* may not feel the need for detailed plans, the company needs an operational framework to provide focus and track progress. Founders can't provide the rationale for their decisions to make their reasoning understood, much less the steps to turn that reasoning into reality. Theory can't translate into practice. There's a disconnect. And when you don't have any plans, what are you left with?

Not much.

Advice: How to Plan, Prioritize, and Focus

Partner with a Manager of Execution.
Lots of successful companies have been built on partnerships that combine visionary founders with execution-focused operators. Think about Mark Zuckerberg and Sheryl Sandberg, Drew Houston and Dennis Woodside, Larry Ellison and Safra Catz, or Steve Jobs and Tim Cook. In each case, the founder brought bold creativity and strategic vision, while their counterpart ensured the business ran smoothly, grounded in operational excellence and consistency. These partnerships balance daring ideas with the practical work of building systems, managing people, and scaling the business.

Rich has been lucky enough to experience this synergy firsthand. When his 360s came back, one name kept coming up: Stacy McKinney. She was the operational yin to Rich's strategic yang, a socially skilled leader who balanced relationships with rigorous execution. Her emotional intelligence, conflict resolution skills, and ability to inspire trust ensured the organization remained cohesive, while her discipline, planning, and practicality ensured they delivered results.

As the company evolved from a consulting firm to a technology-enabled business, Stacy ensured they had the systems and processes to scale effectively. As COO, she brought order to Rich's chaos. She empowered the team, executed the strategy, and gave Rich the freedom to focus on innovation, coaching, and client relationships. Every few weeks, Rich would come to her with a wild idea, and she would respond with a predictable script: "Where does this fit into our strategic plan?"

It was a beautiful relationship of counterbalances and complementary skills. Find one of your own.

Identify the key drivers of value creation for the organization.

Where is the gold being mined? Is it your lifetime value/customer acquisition cost (LTV/CAC) ratio, your revenue growth rate, your revenue churn rate, your incremental gross margin percentage, your net retention, your go-to-market speed? Find your golden numbers, then be sure you are keeping your employees relentlessly focused on them. But metrics alone won't do it. You must clarify how you will impact these metrics and what projects and initiatives will enable it.

Set clear objectives.

Every task or project should have a clear objective. For example, if you plan to launch a new product, define what success looks like—reaching a certain number of sales, getting featured in industry publications, or receiving positive customer feedback. Having clear objectives helps guide your planning process and provides a benchmark to measure success.

Next, communicate the goals and the reasons behind them to your team. Encourage their feedback and make sure they understand the "why." This helps the team buy into the goals and could highlight any unrealistic expectations. Foster a culture that supports learning, progress, and taking risks. If the team feels secure in trying to achieve stretch goals, they will be more likely to reach for them.

Put cadence into your calendar.

Cadence is crucial to planning. It brings both flexibility and discipline. Interrogating your priorities regularly gives you the flexibility to make adjustments when needed. But it also makes sure that those priorities are monitored and executed! What do you do annually, quarterly, monthly, weekly? How often do you hold leadership meetings? How often do you hold all-hands meetings? Depending on the project, do you have weekly, monthly, or quarterly OKRs to hit? These will change as the company grows, but regular meetings give you crucial reference points. As long as they have clear agendas and takeaways, they ensure everyone is on the right track and negotiating problems as a team.

Rank everything, all the time.

> The key is not to prioritize what's on your schedule,
> but to schedule your priorities.
> —Stephen Covey[1]

Everything needs to be ranked: important or not important, urgent or not urgent. The important and urgent stuff gets done first. The important and non-urgent stuff gets done later. The unimportant and urgent stuff gets delegated, and the unimportant and not urgent stuff gets deleted.

The first question that Rich asks his founders is: "What are you focusing on today?" because it instills a sense of prioritization. For many years, he had a Post-it note on his mirror that said: "What is the most important use of my time today?" Founders face an array of tasks, all seemingly urgent and important, but a successful entrepreneur understands the necessity of distinguishing the critical from the non-critical, the immediate from the non-immediate. You need to *stop* equating busyness with productivity, confusing efficiency with bureaucracy, and neglecting to delegate. You need to *start* focusing on impact, using prioritization frameworks, and aligning team efforts.

Start prioritizing your work based on the impact of your goals.
**Every action that does not bring the company
closer to its goals is not productive.**
—Eliyahu Goldratt[2]

What are the most important things you must do to achieve your strategic objectives? Focus on *those* things and don't get sidetracked by less important tasks. Each task in your list should be evaluated based on its impact on your startup. A practical way to approach this is by asking, "If I could only accomplish one thing today, what would make the biggest impact on my company?" That's your most important task. For instance, if you're in the early stages of your startup, acquiring new customers might be your top priority, so tasks related to sales and marketing should take precedence over others.

Learn to say no.
Founders get excited about possibilities and fear missing out on new opportunities. So, when an interesting new prospect pops up, they get excited and want to pursue it. But you can't do everything, so you must learn to say no to new opportunities that don't align with your priorities.

When founders say yes to new opportunities that aren't aligned with their priorities, it can damage their company in several ways. First, it can lead to scope creep, when a project or product starts to grow beyond its original scope. This leads to delays, budget overruns, and, ultimately, failure. Second, it can lead to a lack of focus, making it difficult for the company to achieve its goals. Third, it can create resentment among employees who feel their work is not valued.

What are the most important things your company needs to achieve in the short and long term? Once you know your priorities, you can start to say no to opportunities that don't align with them. Be realistic about your resources. How much time, money, and staff do you have available? Don't commit to more than you can realistically deliver.

Learn the art of following through.

This is about driving *organizational* focus. Even the best-laid plans can fail without regular monitoring and follow-up, leading to missed milestones, delayed progress, and all sorts of opportunity costs. Radio silence can demoralize employees, disrupt team cohesion, and generally undermine trust and credibility: "Lots of internal projects tend to kick off with all kinds of energy and exclamation marks, but then they inevitably fizzle out into nothing."

It's incredibly important to regularly monitor progress against plans so you can adjust if things are getting off track. The idea is to identify potential problems early on and take corrective action before they become major issues. Take advantage of project management tools. Talk to people. Look out for missed targets.

Finally, be lazy.

What does a lazy person want? Only one job to do. Your job is to identify and remove the biggest constraint. Find the biggest bottleneck and fix it. Then move on to the next one. Avoid the "Everything, Everywhere, All at Once" syndrome. Jim Schleckser sums up the problem in his book *Great CEOs Are Lazy*:

> A lot of the mediocre and hardworking CEOs we have run into over the years are exceptionally good at what we call "peanut buttering." When it comes to allocating their time to the various tasks and stakeholders in their businesses—their boards, their supply chains, their investors, their communities, etc.—these CEOs do their best to spread their time as evenly as possible across all of them. The concern, of course, is to make sure everyone feels like

they're getting the CEO's attention. In this effort, the CEO will work very hard, sometimes as much as eighty or more hours a week. The bad news is that this is the surest way possible to dilute the CEO's impact on any one issue. Unfortunately, this concept of tending to every stakeholder is taught at many major business schools, which only perpetuates the error. This is done, in part, because CEOs aren't certain what actions will drive the business forward; consequently, they work on all fronts, hoping one will yield results.[3]

Death by peanut butter! Founders constantly struggle with balancing long-term vision and day-to-day problems. How do we know this? Because that's what their colleagues say: "Everything is reactive with him. He's constantly responding to things, he's never driving things forward, much less responding to the things that really matter."

■ ■ ■

Planning, prioritizing, and maintaining focus mark the difference between drowning in the daily persecutions of startup life versus charting a course *through* those challenges toward attaining your strategic vision. It provides *tactical* direction by clearly communicating focus in terms of roles, targets, responsibilities, and goals. It keeps the lights on and ensures the business operates smoothly in the present. It is the daily practice of effective execution.

CHAPTER 12

The Art of Hiring: Finding and Attracting Talent

W ho was one of Marc Benioff's first hires at Salesforce? Nancy Connery, the legendary HR manager who recruited over 650 employees, many of whom are still with the company today. She was one of three people he brought over from Oracle when he founded the company in 1999. In his great book *Behind the Cloud*, Benioff writes, "We take hiring as seriously as we do revenue. Some people say I am obsessed with hiring, and they're right." When Tien cold-emailed his resume to jobs@salesforce.com, he got a call from Nancy the next day.

Tien, in turn, eventually took hiring very seriously at Salesforce. And he was very good at it. At one point, he realized that with each person the people he was hiring were better and better. And as a result, they were making him better. So when he started Zuora, he decided to continue the pattern. One of his early hires was Rene Cirulli, a brilliant recruiter and talent scout. They were off and running.

But then, a series of unfortunate events happened. Three, in fact.

Here's the first event. Tien is personally impressed with a potential sales executive, so he invites them to a group dinner. Before they leave the dinner, the prospect says, "Well, I'll leave you all to your decision now, but I just wanted to summarize the main messages I heard from everyone at the table." They proceed to do exactly that, person by person. They wow everyone. The team agrees: let's hire this person. Six months later, this same sales executive is eating everybody alive. They are completely toxic. The situation is akin to throwing a piranha into a goldfish tank. They were a very canny sales executive, and Tien got sold.

Second event. Tien makes a big hire, but then starts questioning his decision. He's wondering if he got sold again. This person isn't toxic, but Tien is wondering if they are actually kind of an empty suit. Then one morning, he reads an article titled "10 Things to Say at Meetings to Make Yourself Sound Intelligent" and realizes that a lot of this material sounds familiar. He's hearing it at meetings from this same person! Another exec confirms his suspicions: This person sure talks a lot, but they're really not saying anything. Yep, Tien got sold again.

Third event. Tien and his CPO, Guillaume Vives, are really excited about a prospective new engineering hire. This person is so good, they decide to make them an offer. "Well," says Guillaume, "we still haven't run them by our board member Peter Fenton." "Don't worry about it," says Tien. "Peter will love them." Later that week, they get a call from Peter: "I talked to that person. I sure hope you didn't give them an offer." Whoops. A year later, the hire is gone.

Three unfortunate events, and you're out.

This is when Tien realized he actually wasn't very good at this. In fact, he plainly sucked at it. Maybe his previous successes were luck. Maybe the game was getting harder. The reason didn't matter—he had to admit, he had a problem. It was actually kind of liberating: admitting you are bad at something actually puts you back in the beginner's mind. And what he learned was hiring isn't something you do by gut. It requires experience. It requires a framework for assessing talent. It requires a disciplined process (involving the rest of his exec team) that really explores and evaluates how people think and behave. But how do you go about doing that?

Why Is Hiring So Hard?

Neglect is a problem. Time, money, and attention are stretched thin, and every hour or dollar needs to be invested wisely. Proper staffing often gets the stepchild treatment, leading to hasty hiring decisions and inadequate onboarding processes. Especially in the early days, all it takes is one bad hire to poison the whole room.

Competency is a problem. Most founders simply don't know how to do it (hire effectively, that is). They lack experience in job analysis—thinking through the skills, knowledge, and experience required to do a specific job effectively. They don't do their homework. They are poor interviewers. They don't cast a wide enough net. They naively trust their gut reaction and make impulsive decisions. They don't listen to other opinions. They don't back-channel. They simply do not know how to do the job of filling jobs.

Upgrading talent is a problem. The people who got you here aren't going to get you there. Lots of people (very good people) can't scale. They are learning on the job and don't have the knowledge or experience to know what to do. They may have a certain attitude and approach that hasn't adjusted to the new demands. They often use a rinse-and-repeat formula. But what works at a $30 million run rate won't work at a $100 million run rate. And when people hit their competency threshold, it's time for an upgrade. It's a sad fact of life. The talent escalator needs to keep moving.

Startup culture is a problem. The long hours, constant uncertainty, and strategic pivots take a toll. Burnout and stress are huge issues. Poaching happens all the time. Not everybody can handle a startup's intensity and ambiguity. When they have other employment opportunities, many employees seek a holistic employment package beyond monetary compensation. When people don't feel valued or heard, they will jump ship.

Competition is a problem. Demand for talent often outstrips supply, particularly in areas like AI, data science, and security. Big companies can offer competitive salaries, robust benefits, job security, and professional development opportunities, which can be attractive to top-tier candidates. What do startups have to offer? A promise.

So, lots of problems. And the founder, of course, sits on top of that list. This might sound counterintuitive. After all, aren't these people full of charm, tenacity, intelligence, and vision? They've attracted some early team members and investors. They're finding real traction in the market. But once the company needs to start attracting more seasoned senior-level employees, everything goes off the rails.

Not a People Person

Hiring is one of those disciplines, like marketing or design, that many founders like to think they (a) understand and (b) are very good at. But it's a full-time profession for a reason. It entails things like understanding the skills and knowledge that are essential for success in any specific role, crafting relevant interview questions, effectively communicating the value proposition of the role and the company, putting the candidate at ease, listening carefully, assessing the relevance and depth of candidates' responses, calibrating culture fit with the need to adapt the job to scaled-up demands, checking references, engaging with stakeholders, and closing candidates.

Recruiting is a career specialty for a reason. People spend decades learning to become skilled talent scouts. There is always new research, new practices, new platforms, new competitive dynamics. Professional recruiters bring a specialized understanding of the talent market so that startups can gain access to a wider, more qualified pool of candidates than founders can find on their own. They apply rigorous screening processes and can objectively assess candidates against the company's needs and culture, a task founders may struggle with due to biases or a lack of experience in hiring. They also efficiently manage the recruitment process from start to finish, allowing founders to focus on strategic growth areas, something that's crucial for startups with limited resources and personnel.

Many founders underestimate the investment of time and strategic thinking required for effective hiring. They mistakenly believe that a robust talent pipeline will self-generate and that the mere presence of skilled individuals will automatically resolve existing challenges. This overlooks the necessity of a detailed job analysis to pinpoint the specific competencies, experiences, and skills vital for achieving desired results. On top of this, they tend to improvise during interviews due to insufficient preparation, leading to a lack of consistency and depth in candidate assessment. So, not surprisingly, they repeat common hiring mistakes and inadvertently compromise their company's potential for long-term success.

They might be able to pitch their vision, but many can be interpersonally clueless. They lack social astuteness. They don't know how to read nonverbal cues. They don't know how to banter. There's a lot of icy silence in the room. They can be much more charming talking to 2,000 people in a conference hall than one person in an interview room. They might be savvy or sharp when it suits them, but they're not always sensitive, courteous, or tactful. Amazingly, they often try to "win" the job interviews they conduct!

Since they like to be the center of attention, they tend to talk more than listen. They are less empathetic and probably don't show much interest in understanding the deeper motivations of candidates. They tend to be quite pessimistic and cynical, which certainly isn't motivating to potential senior candidates. They are far from diplomatic and are more likely to come across as blunt, critical, unpleasant people. What's not to love?

The end result? A cascade of opportunity costs: missed candidates, missed ideas, missed alignment, missed direction.

Building the Process

When we look at our database of founders, those who are good at finding and attracting talent get *dramatically* better results than those less effective at hiring. They are more reflective and disciplined about the whole process. Even though they still have a high sense of urgency, they take the time to dig into the complexity of people and problems and end up with much deeper insights. They are less likely to feel comfortable with the status quo and are more comfortable with making changes in their organization and looking for different ways of doing things. As a result, not only are they more motivated to upgrade the talent on their team, but they are driven to surround themselves with the sharpest people they can find who share their values.

They are much better at promoting their company because they genuinely love their job. They are skilled at creating meaning and helping candidates see how the company is trying to make a dent in the universe. This kind of inspiration attracts people to their company. Not only are they deeply engaged in the hiring process (they win particular plaudits for their negotiation skills), but they recognize the value of understanding the intricacies of building teams and partnerships. They take the time to involve their teams in hiring and get their buy-in on important hiring decisions. At the same time, they are considered much more objective, emotionally controlled, and inclined to make fact-based decisions. They can make hard calls about early employees when they need to.

So what happened to Tien after he struck out (at least) three times? He decided to build a process. He knew he was a good synthesizer and interpreter, so he decided to build an interview committee. He enlisted the help of some board members and investors. He had them interview his candidates first, then got them all in a room and listened to their opinions.

The best part was when they disagreed. Why? It was a great way to learn about team priorities and get different perspectives on candidate aptitudes, the true demands of the role, and the team dynamics. Crucially, this was the discussion where the real subject matter experts could share their thoughts on the relative capabilities of the candidate. So, by the time the candidate talked to Tien, it was a much broader conversation: who they are, how they think, what motivates them, what's the next step in their career journey.

Advice: How to Find and Attract Talent

Recognize that you are not good at this.
Founders are generally abysmal at interviewing people. Some of them are standoffish at best and downright robotic at worst. They frequently

blatantly telegraph what they're looking for: "Well, we need somebody who will do this and this. You're like that, right?" They often forget they are there primarily to *listen* instead of talk. Sometimes, candidates can't get a word in edgewise.

Our primary advice for interviewing? Stick to the facts and focus on understanding the candidate's past behavior. Avoid vague hypothetical questions ("Let's say you were in the following scenario . . ."). Stay concrete. Interrogate actual situations, not theoretical constructs. Interrogate lived experiences: Why did you do this project? Who did you work with? What was the actual versus expected outcome? What were the biggest obstacles? What was your organizational structure? How did you interact with your cross-functional peers? There are no right or wrong answers; you're just trying to get a sense of the person by how they respond. Their character will reveal itself.

Develop a disciplined hiring process.

Have a disciplined hiring process you don't violate: writing job descriptions, sourcing candidates, interviewing, following up, reaching decisions, etc. It should also include soliciting and synthesizing feedback from multiple references: team members, board members, and shared contacts. Utilize data-driven hiring tools like personality testing to improve fit and retention. Use a strict process for surfacing information about people to ensure that the facts always win. It's human nature to seize on commonalities and shared experiences, but those affinities can often obscure competency gaps.

For example, Tien is maniacal about job scorecards to keep interviews focused on skills, knowledge, and experience rather than just whether you like someone. In other words, have a detailed description of what the role entails: its context, its objectives, its challenges, its scope, and what you need the person to be able to do and accomplish. For important roles, he writes around a half dozen drafts: writing, leaving it for a day, rewriting, etc. And the best candidates? When they see the final scorecard, their eyes light up. They get excited. They can see themselves in the role. They see the future of their own story, their own growth.

Diversify the gene pool.

You need to reach beyond your own network. You need a wider net. This is where your investors and board members can contribute, particularly for young founders. It marks the difference between essentially posting a classified ad ("WANTED: VP OF PRODUCT") and taking advantage of a range of experienced perspectives to help locate a specific suite of skills.

You might also want to consider hiring a recruiting firm. Be careful, though, because a lot of these are glorified temp firms. Look for a company that doesn't just reach for low-hanging fruit. Look for one that invests in understanding not only the job specifications but the culture fit issues. They need to conduct a thorough search to try to find people who fit exactly what you need. Find the pros instead of the folks who are just dialing for dollars.

Hire for the team, not the position.

You can't put together a good basketball team with five all-star forwards. It's the *chemistry* of the team that is going to create success. Founders tend to hire in a silo. They want the best salesperson. They want the best engineer. They want the best marketer. And they wind up with a bunch of big egos that can't work together.

At a certain point, you're going to need more experienced people. The biggest problem in bringing in these hires is that their experience has allowed them to develop clear models of the "right way" to do things. If they have spent a long time at a single company (big or small), they may try to simply repeat past formulas. They will likely be more balanced if they have worked at multiple companies at various stages of growth (and also have different industry or market segment experience).

The big company hire is another kind of challenge. If they were around during the growth and scaling of that company, they can appreciate the lack of systems, processes, and structure of a startup. But if they joined their previous company when it was at a more advanced stage (or if they joined a big company that was in either expansion stage or continuous growth), they will have real difficulty adjusting to the informal, unstructured nature of a startup. They may tell themselves and tell you that they will enjoy the challenge of a more dynamic startup, but they tend to be judgmental and thrown for a loop by the ambiguity and chaos and label it as "naive." As a result, the antibodies (your early employees) attack them as "big company" people and don't benefit from their scaled-up models and processes.

Practice extreme backchanneling.
Backchanneling is incredibly important. If you can't find information about someone through your own network, cold-contact people who used to work with the candidate. Again, don't ask fuzzy questions like: "Would you hire this person again?" or "How was your experience with X?" Focus on the details: What specifically did this person do? How did they work with other people? What specific challenges did they face? What specific outcomes did they generate? Let your job scorecard guide your questions. Just because they came from a successful company doesn't mean they were in a role where they "made it happen." Sometimes, they just watched it happen, and sometimes, they had no idea it was happening at all. Sometimes, they actually *resisted* it happening. Be sure you find out what role they played.

Why is this so important? Well, some people are very skilled interviewers. Marketers know how to tell a good story. Salespeople know how to pitch. You might have someone who dazzles throughout the entire process but is fundamentally unfit for the role. You need to listen to others who have worked with the candidate in question. Their responses will tell you volumes. For example, you might get what Larry David calls a "non-recommendation recommendation," in which an ex-coworker damns the candidate with faint praise.[1] That's always a red flag.

Ask yourself: Am I buying or selling?
Interviews aren't just about assessing candidates. They're also about selling the company: the vision, the market, the funding, the product, the team. Experienced candidates have many options and weigh these fundamentals very carefully. They want to kick the tires. Founders who are

good at hiring understand that they are operating within a broader competitive landscape.

Ideally, every interviewer in the process should have a specific competency to evaluate so there's as little redundancy as possible. So, when the founder arrives, the interview is more of a shared conversation than an interrogation. Rich has seen founders who conduct interviews like police officers in old movies, working in dark rooms with table lamps. That's no way to attract talent.

Here's a simple way to think about it: When you're buying, you're listening, and when you're selling, you're talking. You need to switch gears at some point: "Are there any questions for me that I can answer?" That's the time to leverage your vision to inspire someone.

Emphasize the dynamic environment and the disruptive nature of your mission and strategy. Let people know that their creativity is valued. This is vitally important if you want to attract people who can tolerate ambiguity and risk because it will give them the flexibility to be innovative.

■ ■ ■

Ultimately, hiring is both an art and a science, requiring vision, empathy, and analytical rigor. But if you invest time and thought into this process, you can avoid all kinds of horrendous mistakes while also attracting talented people who truly align with your mission and values. By recognizing your own limitations, leveraging external expertise, and building a structured approach, you can cultivate a workforce that not only drives results but also bonds together in spirit and collaboration. You can build a team of happy warriors.

CHAPTER 13

Team Building: The Founder's Role in Creating an Exec Team

> My model for business is the Beatles. They were four guys who kept each other's negative tendencies in check. They balanced each other, and the total was greater than the sum of the parts. That's how I see business: great things are never done by one person; they're done by a team of people.
>
> —Steve Jobs[1]

> None of us is as smart as all of us.
>
> —Ken Blanchard[2]

A few weeks into his work with Tien, Rich suggested a company-wide culture survey. Tien was less than enthusiastic. Oh great, another survey. It felt like busy work. But he had made a commitment to his board to figure things out with Rich, so he reluctantly agreed. When the results came back, they were rough: departments were fighting like cats and dogs, the right hand didn't know what the left hand was doing, everyone thought that management was sitting in an ivory tower, and every day brought a new ugly spat. While the employees generally agreed with the overall strategy, they were losing confidence in the ability of the company to achieve it.

Tien struggled with how to respond to the survey results. He simply didn't know where to begin. Should he commission a formal corporate culture document? Should he schedule more skip-level meetings? Would more off-sites help? How do you go about solving a problem like culture? He was pretty sure scheduling more meetings wasn't the answer, but he was at a loss.

Then, after a particularly frank conversation with Rich, it clicked. Tien had his eureka moment. He had been focusing on the symptoms instead of the disease. He had only one thing he needed to do. He needed to learn how to build a team.

Why Are Teams Important?

By understanding the patterns of interaction within a team, we can predict the team's productivity and creativity. It's the interactions that make the team, not just the smarts or efforts of individual members.
—Alex Pentland[3]

Most founders have learned about the value of teams (at least in theory). They help you move faster. They make you more nimble. A truly high-performing team guided by its own shared "decision-making operating system" ultimately helps you speed up, not slow down.

Good teams also provide a sense of collective security. Working in a startup can be brutal. There are market dynamics that are simply beyond your control. There are huge challenges that you simply can't handle alone. Threats lurk around every corner. Knowing that people have your back means a lot.

They give you a cultural foundation. An early-stage startup is an informal family. It sets the tone for a broader corporate culture that will evolve as the startup grows. That culture needs to change and grow, of course (lots of founders fall in love with the good old days and stick by early hires at their peril). But a strong early team provides a very real and special DNA that will endure as the company scales.

They help you work smarter. When you only have a few chances to get it right, you need to be judicious with your time, money, and talent. When a team has figured out how to work and solve problems together, there's much less redundancy and time wasting. A smooth-running machine generates *more* efficiencies as it grows, not fewer.

Good teams also improve your decision-making. There are some calls that only a founder should make, and there are thousands that they shouldn't. Think of a team as a counterweight to bias and ego—an 800-pound brain at your disposal. Smart teams are constantly tuning their decision-making process, learning what issues are truly important, identifying rabbit holes to avoid, and prioritizing accordingly.

They make you more valuable, literally. They increase your investment appeal. VCs are betting on teams that can truly persevere, outwit, outplay, and outlast. They are quick to identify dysfunction and pathology. They'll figure it out if a team is built more on *Hunger Games*–style competition than *Lord of the Rings*–style collaboration.

Finally, you can't scale without them. As the founding team evolves beyond its early undifferentiated blastocyst phase, it needs to bring in more experienced, specialized roles. Smart founders enable that process by clarifying roles and responsibilities and setting up clear organizational lanes so their startup can grow efficiently. They lay down the gridwork needed to reach the next inflection point. Then they do it again.

All of these attributes of teams are true: agility, security, collective intelligence, investment appeal, scale.

But they're not what this chapter is really about. This chapter is about how a founder's company can succeed or fail based on how the founder approaches building their executive team.

So Teams Are Important. So What?

The early days of a startup are essentially a benevolent dictatorship. You're the founder. It's your vision. You raised the money. You convinced the early talent to join up. As a result, getting things done is easy. You just tell people what to do, or you do it yourself. You draw up the product design. You sell the first customers. You decide where to spend the money. You bark the orders, and they happen.

But one day, rest assured, things will stop working. You will hit the wall.

Both Rich and Tien have talked to countless founders who say the same thing: A few months ago, all of a sudden, the company seemed to stop working. Everyone started complaining about *everything*: the culture, the strategy, the execution (or lack thereof). Sometimes it happens at 30 people, sometimes at 70. Tien made it to around 120 employees before he hit the wall.

Why is this happening? Because as the company grows, new management layers appear. Tien remembers a conversation he once had with a founder who said he was thinking about hiring an HR leader. He had 30 employees, and all the usual cracks were starting to show. Tien thought that a headcount of 30 was kind of early to hire an HR person, but it turns out this founder had just installed his first management layer. The only problem was that he was still trying to run his company like an eight-person team.

At some point, the benevolent (or not so benevolent) dictatorship no longer works. Once you start gaining traction, the focus shifts to scaling operations. Now your team needs to be adept at managing increased workloads, entering new markets, and handling more complex business operations. Efficiency is key. A skilled team will develop the processes that allow your startup to grow without compromising the quality of your product.

At this point, you are hiring seasoned executives to run big parts of the company: a strong sales leader, an experienced engineering leader who knows how to keep the trains running on time and the system stable, a finance leader that knows how to manage cash, bring down DSO, and run an effective budgeting process.

You would think all these experienced, seasoned execs would know how to work together well. Sadly, that's rarely what happens. Remember, these are successful people with ideas of their own. What's it like to manage a bunch of them? Picture a stagecoach conductor cracking his whip, and every horse running off in its own direction. Tien's team was full of dysfunction, and that dysfunction was *cascading down through the entire organization.*

This is when good, loyal employees start to complain. The departments are being given different goals by your exec team and start to fight like cats and dogs. People become frustrated when the work they are trying to do is blocked, and start to blame the culture, or the "ivory tower." Confidence in the strategy and the company start to erode.

A good exec team is critical for a well-functioning organization. It turns out that teams are only as good as their leader. And for your execs, that leader is you, the founder.

What a Good Team Looks Like

The strength of the team is not each individual member.
The strength of each member is the team.
—attributed to Phil Jackson

As previously discussed, most founders are lone-wolf types. They're generally skeptical of group effort. They weren't on the high school football, soccer, or basketball team. They didn't get mentored by a sports coach, or witness that skilled coach develop real camaraderie. They've never truly experienced it themselves.

Tien fit this profile perfectly. But he was willing to learn. So when Rich told him that learning how to build teams was a skill set he needed to focus on, he got to work. Rich started by asking Tien's executive team to answer a Team Assessment Quiz. We've summarized it here:

- We have the right team composition: right talent, experience and expertise.

- We have a clear purpose and direction and full commitment to the plan.
- We have a strong shared sense of identity, values, and norms.
- We expect collaborative, supportive behavior.
- We have developed an atmosphere of trust and psychological safety.
- We have clear roles and responsibilities.
- We are skilled in working through conflicts and differences of opinion.
- We have direct and open dialogue about critical issues.
- We have active cross-functional teamwork.
- We value the contributions of all team members.
- We empower members who take initiative, solve problems, and make decisions.
- We have a disciplined decision-making process that reduces bias and surfaces critical ideas and facts.
- We enjoy wide, active participation and sharing and building on others' ideas.
- There is individual, mutual accountability between members and team accountability.
- We have high standards of excellence that are clearly defined and monitored.

If you're a founder, we encourage you to take a moment and write down how your team would answer each one of these statements: yes, maybe, or no. If a third of them are nos or maybes, then you don't have a well-functioning team. Needless to say, Tien's team got a failing grade.

It was time to return to first principles. Tien became a voracious reader of team-building books. The two that continue to stand out for him (based on Rich's recommendation) are *The Five Dysfunctions of a Team* by Patrick Lencioni and *Teamwork: What Must Go Right/What Can Go Wrong* by Carl Larson and Frank M. J. LaFasto. If he were to boil them down to a few key principles, they would be the following:

The first principle is *purpose*. Any truly effective team needs to figure out why it exists in the first place. They need to ask themselves the fundamental questions: Why are we here? What is our purpose for being? How are we going to change the world? Larson and LaFasto call it a "Clear and Elevating Goal." Your exec team needs to have a clear sense of purpose before they commit to a plan that will realize that purpose. Without a concrete reason for existence, team members won't feel empowered enough to take initiative, solve problems, and make decisions. They won't have a sense of mission. They will focus on immediate outputs, not broader outcomes.

The second one is *composition*. You need the right people on the bus, but they also need to be sitting in the right seats. If the right mix of talent isn't in the right set of clearly defined roles, then the entire effort is a nonstarter. However, this mix needs to change at different stages, so the trick is to adjust the team to the circumstances of the moment without undermining the entire effort. Teams can get warped in all sorts of ways. They can skew toward a dominant expertise (or way of thinking), or they can be missing a crucial skill set without realizing it. You need a balanced lattice of talent to propagate open dialogue, cross-functional cooperation, and hybrid thinking.

The third component is *safety*. Disagreement should never be career limiting. While divergent thinking is important, people need to share a strong sense of support from the squad. People need to feel free to speak their minds. They need to operate in an atmosphere of psychological safety built on a strong expectation of collaborative and supportive behavior—a place where praise is public and criticism is private. When people are afraid of getting publicly carved up or humiliated (a situation that is all too common at many well-known companies), they close down, stop sharing, and cripple the mission. That kind of toxic environment ripples through the entire organization.

That safety, in turn, creates trust. Trust in the integrity of your leadership and trust in the competency of your team members. There are lots of perfectly fine people who make much better friends than work colleagues. Trust also means knowing that people have your best interests at heart and aren't being manipulative or lazy or passive-aggressive or some delightful combination of all three. Trust isn't something that gets checked off on day one—it often comes from being in the foxhole and surviving a crisis by working together (a crisis might help build character, but it mostly *reveals* it).

The final element is *accountability*. Accountability doesn't just mean pointing out others' missteps; it also means calling out your own mistakes and taking responsibility. The team is there to execute. It needs to operate under high standards of excellence that are clearly defined and monitored. It must run on an "operating system" with a disciplined decision-making process that reduces bias and surfaces critical ideas and facts.

When someone doesn't deliver or gets favorable treatment, it corrodes everything. The old saying about the weakest link in the chain comes to mind. People need to feel like they're working with professionals who are executing to the best of their abilities and hitting their marks. If the team doesn't deliver (even when it consists of the nicest people in the world), it's a failure.

For Tien, this was a lot to take in. On the positive side of the checklist, he could recognize that his team shared a lot of his own personal attributes: clear purpose, autonomy and initiative, frank communication, and high standards of excellence. On the negative side of the ledger, there were obvious gaps in mutual support, psychological safety, and conflict resolution.

He knew that this was going to take a lot of work. Team building was going to be his full-time job going forward. But at least now he had a *framework*, a path forward. And slowly but surely, instead of *dysfunction* cascading down through the org chart, he began to see *synergy*.

Advice: How to Build Strong Teams

Create authentic synergy by listening more and talking less.

Tien used to have a standard approach to meetings: "All the answers were in my head, and I just had to tell people what to do. So my team meetings were essentially lectures. And when other people had the chance to talk, they politely let me finish and then took the opportunity to say their own point. Everyone took turns grandstanding, without really listening to each other. And then the hour was up. Useless. Nothing got done."

Tien knew that any change had to start with him. "For a couple of weeks, I told myself I was only allowed to ask questions. No statements. It was really hard. It was a lot of 'What do you think of what so-and-so just said?' or 'Does anyone agree or disagree?,' which felt extremely awkward at first." But suddenly, Tien remembers, people really started to open up. They started listening to each other, and actually solving problems—or at least identifying the correct ones to figure out.

Think of your team as a problem-solving machine. Don't try to have the answer to everything. Start delegating tasks to encourage initiative and build trust in your people's capabilities. This will allow you to focus on strategic initiatives while your team handles the operational responsibilities.

Give your team real autonomy. Most of the answers to your company's problems are inside the room, but you must give people decision-making authority to build a sense of ownership and arrive at smarter solutions much more rapidly. Empowered teams are more engaged and proactive— they're much closer to the problems, which means they're much closer to the answers.

On a broader level, others must help shape your vision and turn it into a strategy. As a company grows, the original vision is almost always modified based on feedback from the market. A founder who tries to control every-thing and doesn't utilize their team can stifle adaptability and growth. You will become a decision-making bottleneck, and your micromanagement will demoralize your team members.

Invest in building personal connections.

People form bonds by *doing things*: meals, activities, projects. For example, Tien makes a point of taking his executive team to dinner once a month. Most of the talk is about family and friends. People recognize their own hopes and struggles in one another. They connect: "You have to get together with your executive team on a consistent basis without any particular agenda. Treat it like exercise, or sleep, or reading. It's not only a legitimately enjoyable experience, it surfaces all sorts of issues that might otherwise get buried. It builds empathy, which then creates insights."

Participation is really important. When colleagues get to know each other as people, there's less infighting and friction. Start actively working on team building to foster stronger bonds and a cohesive work environment. It's a good way to break down barriers and enhance collaboration. A united team with a strong rapport can weather challenges more effectively.

Do things that build bonds between yourself and your team members. Social events are fine, but you'll notice that most team-building exercises you've participated in probably involve some kind of group activity. You have to build personal connections and relationships with your team members *so they can then invest in building connections with each other.* Some founders are much more socialized than others, but you can't be distant or "too cool for school" when building a team that executes.

Model the behavior you want to see.

Start recognizing individual achievements and celebrating team successes. It's not hard to do and helps build a culture of appreciation and high performance. Psychologists call this "successive approximation," or the process of reinforcing steps of desirable behaviors that are getting closer to the target behavior. People need signals. Reward the kind of activity you want to see in the world.

"This was something I really learned from Rich," says Tien. "I'm not a real rah-rah cheerleader type. But when I recognize people for really executing or figuring out a big problem, then they're much more willing to share (a) how they did it and (b) the other obstacles they're facing. So now we're operating from a place of positivity and creativity when we look at the next problem to unpack."

This is not just a "nice thing to do"—an apathetic or negative work environment will directly impact your bottom line. Regular recognition motivates people and creates a safe environment for them to experiment with new ideas. It builds a culture where effort and results are valued, encouraging team members to continue performing at their best.

This doesn't mean you should throw out negative feedback altogether. It's imperative to offer constructive criticism when someone veers off course. But a little goes a long way. In fact, the *Harvard Business Review* studied this dynamic in high-performing teams and suggested an average ratio of five or six positive comments to one negative one(!).

Empower your team with clearly defined roles and responsibilities.
You have to assign clear roles and responsibilities, understanding that those functions will change as your company matures. Lots of startup employees aren't sure what they're actually supposed to be doing. It's not their fault because their roles haven't been clearly defined. You're setting your people up to fail when you don't assign clear remits. Work tends to flow to the biggest egos, and power dynamics prevail. And as the *Harvard Business Review* observes, clearly defined roles are crucial for smart decision-making:

> The most important step in unclogging decision-making bottle-necks is assigning clear roles and responsibilities. Good decision makers recognize which decisions really matter to performance. They think through who should recommend a particular path, who needs to agree, who should have input, who has ultimate responsibility for making the decision, and who is accountable for follow-through. They make the process routine. The result: better coordination and quicker response times.[4]

When expectations are clear, your team members can focus on delivering their best work without ambiguity. It's the surest way to avoid infighting and confusion.

Build a palette of complementary skills.
It's important to fill your team with people who *complement* your talents, not replicate them. The founders who only hire various versions of themselves are setting themselves up for failure. For example, Rich was once asked to do a Myers-Briggs analysis of an executive team that was *entirely* composed of INTJ personalities—"architects" who were relentlessly

curious, creative, and individualistic. The CEO had essentially duplicated himself half a dozen times. His team wound up creating an exotic piece of hardware that no one wanted, and they burned a huge pile of VC investment in the process.

The fundamental balance is often between relationships and execution. After working with Rich for 18 months, Tien hired more relationship builders on his executive team, as a way to complement his natural execution strengths. He realized that he needed a leadership team who understood how to manage *people*, not just tasks. Crucially, however, he asked these leaders to put managers of execution underneath them who could scale the systems and processes needed to scale a fast-growing company. As a founder, you will need to compose your own balance of talents (this, by the way, is yet another process that never ends).

Always be upgrading your talent.

It's a sad truism that roles tend to outgrow people. At certain inflection points, you will need to up-level your team. Think about new management layers, for example: One layer generally tops out at eight people (the founder and their direct reports), two layers at around 57, three layers at around 400, etc. The math here is rough, but the point is very clear: an organization with three layers of management operates completely differently from an organization with two layers (which operates differently from a single layer org).

The difference in scale is profound. This affects *everything*, from how you communicate, to the increased need for role clarity, to how often you conduct all-hands meetings. But it's especially true for the skills you need on your executive team. Being a second-level manager is simply different than being a first-level manager or a third-level manager.

The scale issue also massively affects how you manage your team. When your directs are primarily third-level managers, for example, you can no longer expect them to know every detail of the company. Instead, your team has to be filled with folks who have seen scale, and your weekly staff meetings need to speak more to building the policies and systems that allow everyone in the company to play their role with passion and efficiency.

When you're a true leader of leaders, you understand that shifts in scale necessitate upgrades in talent and experience.

■ ■ ■

When do you know if you've built a healthy executive team? When your direct reports genuinely enjoy working with each other. When they can finish each other's sentences. When the presentations they give to their own teams are aligned around shared goals, not pet initiatives. When they call each other up directly to solve issues, versus bringing the problem to the principal's office (i.e., you). When those issues can be addressed respectfully and resolved effectively. When failure is collectively owned as much as success. When they know how to call on each other's strengths, and have the trust to do so. When everyone can feel real synergy, that strange unseen force that elevates the collective effort of a group into a result that is far greater than the sum of individual contributions. When everyone benefits from mutual support, creativity, and shared purpose, and you have the numbers to show for it. That's when you have a real team.

CHAPTER 14

Mastering the Execution Triangle: Delegation, Accountability, and Coaching

A visionary founder of a successful computer company turns into an operational nightmare as the company scales. He is eventually fired by his board, who replaces him with a proven, corporate CEO. Ten years later, as the company continues to struggle (so much for sober professionalism), the prodigal founder returns to lead his company to unparalleled levels of success.

This, of course, is the story every founder knows of how Steve Jobs came back to Apple to save the day. It's the same story they cite to validate the importance and uniqueness of the founder, and to justify their own behavior and thinking. But it's missing the most important chapter: the wilderness years that Job spent between his Apple tenures, and the lesssons that he learned.

Jobs changed *profoundly* during that time. After he got fired, he was supremely confident that he could simply duplicate his early success at Apple with a new computer company, NeXT. Of course, it's never so easy. The NeXT computer was a brilliant machine with cutting-edge hardware, but it had zero compatibility and cost $6,500 in 1988 (around $15,000 today).

There was simply no market for it. It was the classic case of an answer in search of a question. As the consultant and columnist Tim Bajarin notes in a *Forbes* article:

> A few friends who worked for NeXT until its demise have told me that in a way, Jobs was humbled by this defeat, and believed he learned some serious life lessons he would need in his second career at Apple.[1]

What were those life lessons? Well, he clearly managed to gain some control over his temper and general volatility. As his old coworkers attest, his management style calmed down significantly—there were fewer tantrums, fewer public humiliations, fewer flying wads of paper. But it was more than that.

> It turned out that one of the life lessons Jobs learned while he was in his wilderness period at NeXT and the years between the closing of NeXT and going back to Apple, was the importance of mentoring and preparing his management team to be less dependent on him. While at Apple in the early days, he micromanaged just about everything related to running the company.
>
> However, when he returned to Apple, he was more willing to delegate responsibility, and more importantly, learned to rely on and trust his top managers.[2]

Delegation? Mentoring? Trust? These aren't words we typically associate with Steve Jobs. If there is a lesson in this story, it's that the Steve Jobs who returned to Apple *was not the same Steve Jobs who got fired from Apple.* He thought he could just create another hit product, and he was wrong. He was humbled by defeat, faced down his demons, and matured as a leader.

Apple would not be the success it is today if Jobs had not learned how to delegate tasks, find the right people to hold accountable, and invest in mentorship and coaching. He spent hundreds of hours in conversation with Tim Cook before handing over the company to him. As Bajarin (who knew Jobs personally) said after talking with him in 1997:

I remember walking away from that meeting shaking my head and questioning who was the guy I just met with at Apple HQ. He was 100% different than the last time he and I had met in person in 1988.[3]

Leadership is not just about barking orders, seeing around corners, or rallying the troops. Yes, these are all things that come naturally to founders, but true leadership is about *getting the most out of people who support your vision*.

And how do you do this? Through the triangle of delegation, accountability, and coaching. The sooner you learn how to master this triangle of power, the sooner you will defuse the time bomb and realize your dream.

Steve Jobs learned this lesson. You can, too.

The Answer to Founder Mode

Here's a scene that plays out hundreds of times every week: an investor sits down with a young founder and says, "It's really simple. You just need to hire great people, then get out of the way." So they follow their advice. They bring in the recruiters. They hire a bunch of smart people. The leadership page on their website is now populated with executives with impressive backgrounds and resumes.

But a few quarters later, many of these same founders suddenly find themselves sitting on top of an organization at war with itself. As Paul Graham notes in his piece on founder mode, they feel like they've ceded control of their company to a handful of fiercely intelligent domain experts who are particularly adept at "managing up." Privately, they'll tell other founders that they feel like they're surrounded by professional bullshitters.

So they react. Airbnb's Brian Chesky remembers feeling like he had to get back "in the details and get very, very hands-on." Some revert back to the bad old days: barking orders, shutting down anything that doesn't involve them directly, operating by "look and feel." They storm through the meetings. But there's only one problem: they're not in charge of a startup anymore. They're leading a growing professional organization. It doesn't make sense to operate like you've just come out of Y Combinator.

Yes, you have very special skills that others lack: you're the spark, the vision, the motivator. It certainly doesn't make sense for founders to act like professional managers. But when it comes to delegation, accountability, and coaching, many founders are blinded by an insidious misunderstanding: they view the process as subtractive, rather than additive. They think it's giving up.

It's not, of course. It's the ultimate force multiplier. It's just that delegation, coaching, and accountability work differently for founders than professional managers. It's a trickier balance. That's what this chapter is about. Steve Jobs didn't bark orders at Tim Cook, but he also didn't let him completely take over a core component of his company.

But let's start with an important point: you need *all three skills to succeed*. Otherwise, you'll be left with a two-legged stool.

The Triangle

At this point, you might be asking yourself: Why is it three skills, not two? Why is coaching even included in this process? Aren't we just talking about finding other people to do things, so you don't have to? Doesn't regular guidance go without saying? Besides, how do you go about coaching someone who knows far more about a given subject than you do?

It turns out that delegation, accountability, and coaching work together as a system. Picture them as a cycle: delegation to accountability to coaching to delegation to accountability, etc. The wheel never stops spinning.

Delegation entails getting a clear understanding of your organization, the strengths and weaknesses of each member of your team, and how they all fit together, so you can be clear on who should do what. Accountability entails being crystal clear about what are the expected outcomes, and the specificity and frequency of measuring those outcomes. The steady cadence of coaching is the *flywheel* that propels the entire cycle forward. Without it, you can easily fall into the founder trap of "set it and forget it" or drive-by delegation. And as we'll learn, there are many ways to effectively coach a domain expert. For example, you don't have to be a technical founder to help guide your head of product in the right direction. You just need to know the right questions to ask.

These three skills in tandem form the essential muscle of leadership, or the ability to get the most out of the people who have bought into your vision. Eventually, all successful founders have to learn how to master the triangle. Without it, you're sunk.

Why Founders Struggle with Delegation, Accountability, and Coaching

Founders are not great at delegating, holding people accountable, or coaching. It's just not a skill set they've been trained to do. In our dataset, founders consistently score up to one standard deviation below the mean on delegation and empowerment, holding people accountable, and coaching. Confession time: Tien scored over one standard deviation below the mean on all three skills.

But if these three skills are absolutely essential for scaling an organization, why are founders so terrible at it?

It starts with one of a founder's worst fears: giving up control. Tien once had a product manager pull him aside and tell him: "You keep asking me to do a job, and then without telling me why you are dissatisfied, you wind up doing everything yourself! It's demoralizing and belittling. You need to give me some space, some autonomy. You're driving me crazy." (That product manager also said: "If you'll let me, I'll help you learn how to be a great manager." That simple sentence changed Tien's life.)

But for lots of founders, giving someone autonomy almost feels like giving up the company: What do these people know that I don't? Is this supposed to be my reward for building a business from scratch? Hand over my startup to a bunch of MBAs? Ultimately, for a founder to learn how to delegate, they have to learn how to exercise control from *off the field*. They need to be the coach, not the quarterback.

Then there are the EQ issues. Many founders shudder at the idea of actually trying to understand someone else's professional strengths and weaknesses, much less offering constructive criticism. When it comes to coaching, they tend to focus on correcting mistakes rather than rewarding successes. Everyone needs constructive criticism, but these founders tend to operate on a basis of all sticks, no carrots: "She does not do a good enough job of rewarding achievement. Informal shoutouts in Slack are a nice touch but have no real bearing." Also, since they're so insular, they tend to play favorites: "He's extremely good at rewarding certain groups of people but it's very clear who his favorites are."

Founders are also notorious for using their comfort with ambiguity as a way to defer and deflect uncomfortable responsibilities. They tend to be vague regarding expectations, unreliable when it comes to following up, and often completely absent when dealing with conflict. They are much happier existing in a world of splendid isolation—of ideas and insights, ambiguities and opportunities. Here's how a new project typically starts: "Does not explain expectations clearly but will either not say anything or use very vague terms."

Many lack the discipline to, as Australians say, "put in the hard yards." These skills depend on cadence—the boring but important work of keeping track, adjusting tactics when necessary, and staying relentlessly focused on the results. Rich, for example, freely admits that he lacked the self-discipline to establish a proper cadence with his employees until he hired a great EA who was a manager of execution. Like many other founders, he was happy to write, do research, and chase down various other personal interests. Founders are often workaholics who manifestly suck at getting actual work done.

Finally, this triangle of skills cannot exist without structure, process, and metrics. These founders hate all those things. They tend to focus on abstract ideas rather than practical, measurable objectives, making it hard to hold their team accountable. In a sense, they are averse to accountability itself: "He is amazing at attracting and hiring talent that he then goes on to neglect completely. Rote accountability dynamics at this company are completely nonexistent."

Without these structures in place, what are you left with? Palace politics. Favoritism. Inconsistent messages. Wobbly standards. Shifting goalposts. Procrastination. Sandbagging. Mediocrity. Inertia. In short, an organizational effort that resembles the worst aspects of its ostensible leader: "Actual achievements are not really rewarded and poor performance can continue for a long time with seemingly no consequences."

If you are a founder and any of this material resonates, there's good news. Delegation, accountability, and coaching are skills that can be learned. Here's a framework to get you started.

Delegation

In their heart of hearts, many founders know the importance of delegation. If you fail to delegate, you will find yourself obsolete, overtaken by your inability to adapt your leadership style to the needs of a growing organization. Delegation also helps prevent founder burnout by distributing the workload, allowing you to maintain your well-being and continue leading effectively. It lets you focus on the strategic priorities determining your company's trajectory, ensuring that you're steering the ship rather than running around plugging leaks.

Effective delegation is also the linchpin of scalability. You can use it to extend your reach, multiply your effectiveness, and grow your startup beyond the confines of your personal capacity. Crucially, however, it also gives you agility. Empowered teams can react swiftly to market changes. If you do it right, your company can become big *and* fast.

Delegation and empowerment signal trust in your team's abilities, encouraging the stars and athletes to grow with the company. They, in turn, serve as a talent pipeline for developing future all-star managers ready to take on greater responsibility as the company grows. It also fosters an environment where innovation and creativity flourish. When team members feel empowered, they're more likely to contribute interesting ideas that can propel your startup forward.

Finally, it instills confidence in your boardroom. Investors like to see robust delegation systems in place, as it demonstrates your ability to build a team and infrastructure that can sustain growth. In essence, delegation is not merely about alleviating the present workload; it's about creating a robust foundation for future growth. It's very simple: without delegation, you will make yourself obsolete.

Again, this all reads fine in theory. But the only real way to learn the value of delegation is to practice it.

Advice: How to Delegate

Evaluate and prioritize your time.
One of the first things that Rich does with a founder is ask them to audit their calendar. You can't learn how to delegate until you first understand how you are spending your time. Identify the tasks that only you can do, and jettison everything else. What are the most important things you must do to achieve your strategic objectives? Focus on *those* things and don't get sidetracked by less important tasks.

Identify tasks to delegate.
Now that you've picked out the most important priorities, what do you do with the rest of the things on your plate? You delegate them! Get rid of those routine tasks. You probably weren't going to make most of those one-on-ones anyway. Now you can schedule much more time for creative thinking and strategic planning. In other words, the important stuff. Defend that white space with your life.

Get to know your team.
Tien once interviewed a potential head of sales who couldn't remember the names of his reps. Needless to say, he didn't get the job. In order to decide who gets what, you have to first take the time to understand your employees' strengths and aspirations, as well as their weaknesses. Lots of Rich's clients lack the ability to objectively evaluate their direct reports. You might

consider using a framework (Myers-Briggs, the Big Five personality test, the Enneagram, etc.) to help you assess the management style of the person you're working with.

Tien liked Rich's leadership framework so much that he had his entire leadership team go through the process of giving everyone a common language to understand each other as leaders. This is where empathy and understanding are also crucial—those who don't understand their employees will waste a lot of time trying to fit square pegs into round holes.

Match tasks to strengths.

Once you understand your team, you are in a position to make sure the right people are handling the right responsibilities. Gather information about someone's performance, identify their strengths and their problem areas, and set developmental goals with your team members. For example, the Three Pillars of Leadership is a good framework to start thinking about what kind of management style is needed for a given task or responsibility.

What if you're still not sure who makes sense for a particular project? Rich likes to ask people to go out and research a particular idea, to "roll around in the problem" for a while, and then report back. It's a way to better understand the issue, gauge and develop the talent, and discover hidden skills.

Determine the appropriate level of delegation.

Balance control and autonomy: Adjust the level of delegation based on the team's maturity and the complexity of the task. As trust and competence grow, move toward higher levels of delegation. Take advantage of the Seven Levels of Delegation:

- **Tell:** The leader makes the decision and informs the team member.
- **Sell:** The leader makes the decision but explains the reasoning behind it to get buy-in.
- **Consult:** The leader seeks input from the team member, considers it, and then makes the final decision.

- **Agree:** The leader and the team member make the decision together through a consensus process.
- **Advise:** The team member makes the decision, but the leader offers advice and support.
- **Inquire:** The team member makes the decision, and the leader follows up afterward to understand the decision made.
- **Delegate:** The team member has full autonomy to make and act on the decision without any oversight.

Accountability

"To really hold people accountable, you have to first be able to define objectives, scope, and goals clearly. I'm not seeing any of that happen at this company." Have you ever heard a similar sentiment from your board? Accountability isn't about being punitive; it's about crafting a transparent, equitable, and efficient environment where everyone understands their expectations and adheres to a shared set of standards. Failure to do so fosters a culture where neglecting commitments is tacitly accepted, paving the way for all kinds of problems down the road. Lose accountability, and you lose the ship.

We all want to work in positive, supportive work environments. But the good vibes aren't going to last long if the numbers are in the tank. As Reed Hastings noted in his famous deck on culture at Netflix, startups aren't a family—they're a team. You need to be careful about inadvertently tolerating mediocrity. As Hastings notes: "Adequate (though not the best) performance gets a generous severance package."[4]

All founders are responsible for creating their own corporate culture, but if that culture doesn't include a widely accepted definition of what accountability means to their startup, then there's really no reason to be doing this in the first place. The discipline you add to your organization with regard to meeting commitments is directly proportional to your ability to scale: "It often seems like we make a decision or find a solution to a problem, but then fail to hold people accountable to that solution or direction."

Advice: How to Hold People Accountable

Clearly define both expectations and authority.
The first step (which most founders skip) for creating a culture of account-ability is taking the time to set clear goals. This means you must first provide a clear explanation of the desired outcomes, deadlines, and any constraints. People need to understand what they must deliver, the quality of work you expect, and the timeline they must meet. They need to be clear about their priorities and how their jobs and performance impact the company's success.

Finally, you also need to set expectations about the level of independence and autonomy you're giving people, particularly around decision-making. This means forcing yourself to be clear on: What decisions do you plan on holding on to? What are the joint decisions? What are the decisions that are theirs to make? So many founders avoid defining these expectations as a result of their comfort with ambiguity. You can't let that happen. This is your job.

Scale up delegation gradually.
Start small. Begin by delegating less critical tasks and progressively move toward delegating more significant responsibilities as trust and compe-tence build. Widen territories. Gradually increase the delegation level as your team demonstrates their ability to handle more complex and impact-ful decisions. Don't just dump a project on someone and walk away. As trust develops, you can transfer bigger responsibilities, which prepare your organization to scale by ensuring that key functions aren't bottlenecked by your direct involvement. Crucially, this is also a way for *you* to learn the process. The ability to continuously improve your delegation and empow-erment strategies can make the difference between a company that plateaus and one that makes it to the next rung of the ladder. Giving up authority is difficult for any founder. Make it a gradual, step-by-step process.

Determine what resources or skills your people need to succeed.
Before you can hold someone accountable, you need to know you have set them up for success. Take away all the potential excuses for failure.

Take time to teach and guide as needed. Be available. You may not have the knowledge to be a domain expert in their area, but you can help them work through problems: Ask probing questions that help them unpack their challenges, consider options that they might not have considered, or examine the potential ramifications of their actions or decisions. If they still need deeper expertise than you can provide, then you can help them identify outside resources that can give them mentorship and guidance.

If you don't provide the right support and resources, and your direct report winds up failing, then who really owns that failure? You do.

Communicate and align on goals.

A lot of the executives you will hire as a founder are more like athletes as opposed to artists. You're the artist; you prefer a blank canvas to express your ideas. But your executives are like athletes who want to understand the rules of the game, and how the points are scored. Then they want to figure out how to excel and win.

What does that mean? It means you need to take the time to set performance goals that are specific, measurable, and realistic. Tien likes to use a scorecard system inspired by the hiring book *Who* by Geoff Smart and Randy Street: the mission defined, the outcomes sought, and the competencies required. These goals should also have clear deadlines, which give you a benchmark for measuring team members' progress. Every direct report needs to have a crystal-clear idea of what you expect. In addition, ask all of your direct reports to share their goals, metrics, and priorities to establish mutual accountability and also establish a cadence of quarterly updates and progress.

Rest assured: If you don't set up the rules, your direct report will establish rules of their own. These are smart, experienced people. They'll fall back on something that worked at their last company. But it might not be what the mission requires.

Coaching

Coaching is the engine of the cycle; the kick that spins the wheel. It's much more than a gentle nudge toward operational efficiency; it's the crucial task of transforming role players into all-stars. Weak or nonexistent coaching manifests as a lack of investment in people, neglect of team development, poor feedback, and hazy expectations. This isn't merely a consequence of a founder's lack of managerial experience. It is also born from an insufficient display of empathy, and a latent inability to view their team members as people to be nurtured, rather than as expendable cogs in a machine.

What do effective coaches do? They gather information about someone's performance, identify their strengths and their problem areas, and set developmental goals with their team members. They develop a cadence of check-ins. They build a trusting, collaborative relationship. A great boss who is an effective coach makes their team members feel valued, supported, and empowered. By recognizing their contributions, providing guidance, and encouraging autonomy, they create an environment where employees are motivated, confident, and engaged in their work.

So what do good coaches do? Sometimes, they ask questions in order to help an executive clarify a problem, and sometimes they offer advice. Sometimes, they don't say much at all, and let their team members talk through an issue. They display a willingness to listen, in order to truly understand. They monitor progress, celebrate the wins, and work through the misses. Crucially, they frame this entire effort as "two people figuring out a problem together."

The reality is that as a startup scales, many of the founding team members won't scale with it. They won't grow as managers and leaders. Many don't have the experience, knowledge, or skill to develop without help. Some of these team members have been committed and loyal contributors to the company's growth, but their roles have simply outgrown their capabilities. However, there are always those who could grow with a little constructive feedback, guidance, praise, empathy, and support. Not everyone will make it, but some might flourish with a little help.

Advice: How to Coach

Monitor progress.
Coaching is about monitoring progress. You need to check in on a consistent basis. Offer constructive feedback. Recognize that your report may not meet expectations immediately but can grow with guidance. Your directive is pretty simple: "These are the outcomes I want. These are the results I expect. You determine how you're going to get them." Then as soon as they've developed a plan of action, you need to check back in and help out on a consistent basis. It's a delicate balancing act: You can't tell smart people how to do their job or they'll leave, but you also can't delegate yourself out of existence.

Bill Campbell, known as "The Coach" in Silicon Valley, frequently asked open-ended questions that encouraged people to think deeply and reflect on their own answers: What do you think is the real issue here? What's holding you back? How are you contributing to the situation? How do you think your team feels? How do you see this playing out? He wasn't a technical subject matter expert, but that wasn't the point. He was brilliant at helping people finding the right solution by asking the right question at the right time.

Resist taking back control.
In order to avoid micromanaging, you have to let go of your need for control. Accept that others may approach tasks differently than you would. Focus on the results rather than the method. Avoid taking tasks back. Resist the urge to reclaim tasks because it might seem faster to do them yourself. This can undermine trust and empowerment. Holding people accountable doesn't mean overdoing supervision and attempting to control every part of an employee's work. Overdoing it can create dissatisfaction, disengagement, and turnover. It also limits the time you have to focus on leadership,

strategy, and other higher-level responsibilities. Constantly hovering over your employees will also drive them crazy. By all means, follow up on a consistent basis, but don't make a habit of ruining someone's day.

Empower decision-making and encourage initiative.

Encourage ownership. Empower your team to make decisions within their delegated tasks. Support risk-taking. Encourage team members to take calculated risks and learn from failures, which is critical for their growth and empowerment. When team members feel empowered, they're more likely to contribute interesting ideas that can propel your startup forward. Empowerment is a key ingredient in building a company culture that values initiative, accountability, and collaboration—traits that are essential for long-term success. Conversely, if you are critical or insensitive when employees make mistakes or miss commitments, you will create a culture of intimidation, where employees don't take risks, lose motivation, and develop soul-killing resentments.

Publicly recognize achievements.

Everyone appreciates a shout-out. Acknowledge contributions. Give public credit for the successful completion of tasks and accomplishments. This boosts morale and reinforces the value of delegation. Celebrate successes. Mark milestones and achievements to keep the team motivated and engaged. If all you focus on are mistakes and problems, people will be less motivated to perform and will feel unappreciated. Even if their performance isn't yet up to your standards, let them know when you see progress and acknowledge the behaviors that are in the right direction. But be specific about the behavior you want to see repeated rather than just saying, "Good job." Say you want to help them "take it to the next level." Force yourself to say nice things to people, even if it kills you.

Reflect and learn from the process.

Review outcomes. After tasks are completed, reflect on what went well and what could be improved in the delegation process. Adjust for the future.

Use these insights to refine your delegation strategies, progressively increasing the empowerment and autonomy of your team.

Let your team teach you. Leverage their feedback. Pay attention to how others are responding to you. Adjusting your behavior based on this input can enhance team cohesion and the ability of your team to function independently. Founders frequently stumble when they seem to be operating on a completely different wavelength. When team members feel understood and supported, they're more likely to take ownership of their work, which is essential for scalability.

■ ■ ■

What did Brian Chesky learn after he spent a couple of years going "Founder Mode" and diving back into the operational plumbing of his company? Something very surprising:

> The more in the details I am, the more time I have on my hands. That's a paradox. And I want to explain that paradox—it doesn't make any sense . . . If you decide to be in the details and get very, very hands-on, like I did, it might be a lot more work for about one to two years . . . But once we turned the corner, suddenly everyone started rowing in the same direction. Suddenly I didn't have to be in meetings anymore, and people would do what I wanted to do if I wasn't there . . . There was less turnover. Before, I would get 10 surprises, and nine were bad. Now, I get 10 surprises and nine are good . . . I had a lot less time on my hands initially, and now I actually, weirdly, have a lot more time on my hands.[5]

Yes, Chesky decided to get much more hands-on after he decided he was losing control of his company. But did that mean taking over everything himself? No. It meant getting everyone back into alignment through the cycle of delegation, accountability, and coaching. So many unsuccessful founders are blinded by an insidious misunderstanding: They view the process as subtractive, rather than additive. They think it's giving up. It's not, of course. It's the ultimate force multiplier.

Once you learn how to apply the execution triangle, you will empower others to fulfill your vision. You will give them the direction and resources they need to succeed. You will find the space you need to take your company to the next level. You will find the promised land.

CHAPTER 15

Seeing the Elephant: Facilitating Conflict Resolution

At the weekly leadership meeting, Product is monumentally pissed off at Engineering, and both are equally irate at Sales. Product says that the engineering quality is garbage. Engineering says Product is giving them shitty specs. Sales says that none of it matters, because the prospects are asking for features that our competitors have but we don't. Product notes to Sales that they spent a lot of time training their damn team, so why aren't they doing a better job selling the features that we do have? Sales tells Product and Engineering that they should both spend some time listening to actual customers, but that's practically impossible because (pointing to Support) the support number is a joke—service calls are taking forever to connect. Support, looking hurt and surprised, insists that the average call wait time is five minutes or less. Sales says that can't be true. Support says that they're looking at the figures right now in a spreadsheet. Sales tells them where they can put that spreadsheet. The room goes quiet.

The founder, who has been quietly observing the entire time, makes a suggestion: Why don't we call the number right now?

This, of course, is a fictional story. If it happened in real life, the founder would not be the calm, collected voice of reason. The founder would be picking a side, or desperately trying to change the topic, or checked out on their phone, or berating everybody, or generally making things worse.

Rich hears it from founders all the time: Why can't people just get along? Why does everything have to be a melodrama? I'm not here to referee playground fights. We have the strategy, we have the OKRs. So why can't people just execute the plan?

What these founders are saying, of course, is that their companies would be much easier to run if there were no employees.

Rich can smell conflict avoidance a mile away. He's always marveled at the central paradox behind these complaints: the aggressive, ego-fueled founder who also happens to be deathly afraid of conflict. It's like when a cartoon elephant suddenly encounters a mouse.

But it's understandable. When you're mission-driven, there's nothing more distracting or annoying than messy human emotions. Getting in the middle of other people's squabbles simply has no appeal. Ideas are sharp and clean and infinitely exciting. You can play with them like Lego bricks. Emotions, not so much. But the only way to turn those ideas into reality is through people. What a curse.

But like it or not, *facilitating conflict resolution is part of your job.* You're going to need to figure it out. You can't pretend that other people don't have egos and volitions of their own. Left unattended, conflict can poison your culture and rip your company to pieces. Conversely, if you learn how to resolve arguments in a mutually beneficial way, you'll be able to surface all kinds of hidden truths. Just like in the parable of the three blind men, you'll help your team see the whole elephant, not the individual part specific to their roles. And in doing so, you'll be able to turn your company into a lively forum of ideas.

If you're the kind of founder who hates this stuff (and most do), the good news is that Rich has developed a proven approach to help leaders overcome their fear of dealing with conflict. If you're interested in learning how to turn a classic founder weakness into an actual strategic advantage, read on.

10 Questions: Facilitating Conflict Resolution

1. Do you avoid addressing conflicts with your team, hoping they'll resolve themselves?

2. When conflict arises, do you find yourself quickly picking sides rather than facilitating a balanced discussion?

3. Are you more focused on winning arguments than finding solutions that benefit the team?

4. How often do you find yourself reacting impulsively to conflict rather than listening and understanding the root issue?

5. Do you have a tendency to sidestep follow-up after a conflict is "resolved," assuming it won't resurface?

6. In team conflicts, do you often feel certain that one person is "right" and the other is "wrong"?

7. Are you inclined to delegate conflict resolution to others, even if you know it's affecting team morale?

8. How likely are you to consider outside perspectives or a mediator when conflicts become intense?

9. Do you believe that showing empathy during conflicts could be seen as a sign of weakness?

10. When there's a disagreement, are you quick to assert your solution without truly understanding all sides?

Founders: Less Than Helpful

As anyone who has read a self-help book knows, the first step to recovery is to admit that you have a problem. When it comes to dealing with conflict, however, lots of founders *aren't even aware that the problem exists*. After all, these are the bold and fearless rule breakers. How could they be afraid of a minor office spat?

Well, let's take a quick test. Think about the last few times you've been in the presence of an "executive disagreement," whether it was just a few snide remarks or a full-blown nuclear meltdown. Now take a minute to answer yes or no to the 10 questions above (be honest!). Okay, if you answered in the affirmative to more than a couple, you probably have a problem dealing with conflict. And among founders, you have lots of company.

How do founders make conflict worse? Rich has a list of grimly predictable behaviors that he sees happen over and over again.

Let's start with our old friend *neglect*. Lots of founders seem to have object permanence issues when it comes to conflict—they think that if they can't see it, then it doesn't exist: "It seems like he tries to avoid conflict as much as possible and only resolves it when it's already too late." The unstated hope is that those involved will be adults and work things out themselves. But unaddressed conflict never really goes away. In fact, it feeds on neglect.

Founders frequently *pick sides.* They look at a conflict as a simple binary choice: Someone is wrong, I just need to figure out which one. This approach never ends well. When you pick sides, you leave one party's issues unresolved, which can lead to resentment, or worse, passive-aggressiveness where the losing side actually seeks to undermine the decision. The gremlin might have fled underground, but it's still there, waiting, lurking. Your job isn't to pick a winner and a loser, but to help both sides to see the big picture, like the blind men and the elephant. *That's* your superpower.

Or they try to win the argument themselves! When confronted with two people engaged in an argument, their instinct is to issue a final judgment, without paying much attention to the particulars of the debate. Also not good: "He often initiates or escalates the conflict. He is poor at driving to consensus when there is a stalemate. Often dictates a final decision supporting his opinion, even when it is not shared by the majority."

Founders are also congenitally averse to *following up*: Was the issue resolved, or did it just go away for a while? Without a constructive cadence of dialogue, it's impossible to know whether the disease was truly cured or just went into remission: "This is another activity that she tends to delegate to her COO. In times where she does get involved, she tries to resolve the effect and not the cause."

Remember, there's a difference between intellectual buy-in and emotional buy-in. You need both. Bad feelings tend to linger, and as the old saying goes, "Resentment is like drinking poison and waiting for the other person to die." The high-EQ founders who are skilled at handling resistance follow up with soft touches like: "How do you feel about the decision?," "Your point was really important," "I know this has a big impact on your original plans, and I appreciate your support," etc. These small efforts go a long way toward smoothing out differences.

Sometimes they decide to get rid of the problem by dumping it on someone else. They delegate the job of resolving the conflict to a trusted Relationship Builder. But as we've learned, those people often aren't that great at resolving arguments themselves. There may be some HR speak–inflected mediation involved, but no one walks away thinking anything actually got figured out.

They don't consider *outside perspectives* and make all kinds of assumptions based on incomplete information. They might assume that both parties are being candid about the situation or have access to the same information, for example. Or that they understand the reasons for the other side's actions, or that they bring the same experiences to the situation. But just because one party is silent or doesn't openly voice disagreement doesn't mean that they really agree. The most articulate party is not necessarily the correct one.

When all else fails, they *steamroll people.* Founders are notorious for conducting public executions. This practice is a cancer. It leads to humiliation, the destruction of trust, and a complete dismantlement of healthy candor: "I've seen him get into heated arguments with people, and it's not always clear who is right or wrong. So now everyone is afraid to speak up and say what's actually on their mind."

Steamrolling people is the worst thing you can do. For founders, it also happens to be the most natural thing to do. Instead, you need to practice *patience, patience, patience.* Don't let your hard-wired habits get the better of you.

What these founders don't seem to understand is that the fish rots from the head. Instead of focusing on who is at fault, they should be focusing on what went wrong and how it can be prevented in the future. They should be creating a culture that emphasizes learning from mistakes, open communication, mutual respect, and constructive feedback.

They need to understand that ideas actually *don't* exist in splendid isolation, like metaphorical Lego blocks. They come from people. And if you learn how to channel negativity and conflict into healthy creative friction, both the ideas and the people will benefit.

So how do you do that?

Advice: How to Resolve Conflicts

Reframe conflict as a positive force.

Rather than running away from it, you need to learn to see the potential of conflict. Now, we're not telling you to create conflict for its own sake. That's a terrible idea. You don't want a culture that pits people or departments against each other. You don't want to let the force of your personality normalize unchecked aggression, group tension, and a general lack of civility. But you need to understand that most conflicts happen because (a) people *care* and (b) there will always be competing needs, ideas, and possible strategic directions.

Think of it this way: In the first phase of the company, everything was in your head. For every decision, you were able to visualize all the possible paths, work through the pros and cons, and choose the best way forward, like Dr. Strange in that Avengers movie. That's your founder superpower at work. But when you're sitting on top of a growing organization, there is simply no way for you to know everything anymore. So instead of relying on your intuition, you need to *externalize* those early internal debates with a group of smart, opinionated people.

Working through conflict and disagreement, then, is what allows your company to make smart decisions and find the best solution. If you learn how to manage differences and surface different perspectives without triggering defensiveness, you can channel conflict into a powerful driver of innovation and alignment. When everyone understands that the goal is to find the best answer to a given problem, then lively debate can be a very good thing. Too many founders look at conflict as an uncomfortable situation to sidestep, as opposed to a crucial component of organizational dialogue.

Recognize the difference between destructive and constructive conflict.
The difference is actually quite straightforward: One kind of conflict is about people, and the other one is about problems. One conflict erodes trust, and the other one builds it. Destructive conflict is rife with personal attacks and power struggles. Constructive conflict is about finding solutions and focusing on shared goals. It's your job as a founder to focus the discussion on issues instead of personalities. When you walk away from the debate, or decide to play favorites, you deepen rifts rather than resolving them. There's no doubt that even during the most productive debates, things can get heated. People can get testy. But the founders who frame conflict as a pathway to resolution rather than a battleground for ego establish a balanced approach to conflict that prioritizes mutual respect and trust. You need to learn how to become a good traffic conductor.

Learn the art of emotional regulation and empathy.
Rich has seen time and time again how crucial emotional regulation and empathy are in resolving conflict. When you lose your cool in a tense situation, it never ends well. The founders who stay calm, even when emotions are running high, create a sense of stability that keeps things from spiraling. Whether you like it or not, you are responsible for the temperature in the room.

Empathy is just as important. Conflict typically unfolds as a process, beginning with a triggering event and progressing through a series of emotional and behavioral responses. The founders who have the empathetic intelligence to recognize these stages can intervene constructively before a minor contretemps turns into a prolonged and dispiriting feud. It also allows you to really listen, understand where people are coming from, and show that you care about finding a true resolution, not just a temporary solution.

Learn how to identify the key sources of the conflict.

People often argue about things that are not really the issue at hand. They are haggling over symptoms, not the disease itself. Rich has seen teams get distracted by trying to solve superficial issues like who owns the Christmas party, rather than realizing that the issue is actually about role definitions and holding on to company traditions. Here are three common sources of conflict:

- **Task conflict:** This happens when people argue about work-related goals, methods, or strategies because they're simply not clear. This leads to things like disagreements over a marketing strategy or a product road map. When the mission is ill-defined, egos fill the vacuum.
- **Relationship conflict:** This is messy, schoolyard humanity. People call each other out during meetings, or they form cliques, or they try to undermine each other in all sorts of depressing ways. Rather than work through their issues, someone decides that they don't like someone else, and everyone loses as a result.
- **Structural conflict:** This can entail someone going around their manager to complain to a higher-up, or complaining about disparities in budgets and resources, or fomenting bad vibes between departments. It can be summed up by the title of the Nirvana song "Territorial Pissings." It's a pernicious mindset that completely disregards the fact that your company can only succeed as a team.

Each of these areas can trigger confusion and tension, especially in a fast-paced and resource-strained environment like a startup. The founders who address the root causes of conflict—such as setting clearer priorities, clearly defining roles, enhancing resource allocation processes, and fostering open communication—can prevent minor disagreements from escalating into nasty, dispiriting spats.

Look for win-win solutions, not empty compromises.

Tien sees it happen all the time: conflict happens when different perspectives on the same situation collide. For example, your sales team is hearing lots of customer complaints. So they conclude that your product sucks. The product team, meanwhile, is hitting their targets and hearing lots of positive reviews. How do you resolve both perspectives?

Here's one way to approach this situation: One side is wrong. Let's identify the losing side. Here's a better way: Both sides are essentially correct, but they need to collaboratively discover a *deeper truth* that explains how these different perspectives can exist at the same time. In this case, maybe the answer lies in better customer service and training.

Note that a win-win solution does *not* mean settling on a "least worst option" compromise. It means a *real answer* that resolves both perspectives. These kinds of issues are easy to figure out when you're small. You can just step in, get the details, make the call, and everyone moves on. When you're a bigger company, and you storm in with an ill-informed decision, the results can be catastrophic. It's your job to facilitate a productive conversation between opposing perspectives that discovers the deeper truth.

Develop healthy conflict resolution habits.

You need to strike a balance between intervention and empowerment when approaching a conflict. Start by acknowledging the elephant in the room (there are several elephants in this chapter). Be open about the existence of a conflict instead of ignoring or downplaying it. This shows your team that it's okay to have disagreements as long as they're discussed and resolved in a reasonable way.

Listen carefully to everyone—approach things with a spirit of inquiry. This demonstrates that you legitimately value their perspectives and are interested in understanding their concerns, not just enforcing your own solution. Rich often recommends starting by talking to each party individually. This allows the founder to understand the perspectives, emotions, and concerns involved without bias. Once the initial groundwork is laid, gathering additional context from neutral team members or reviewing work outputs can provide a more objective understanding of the conflict's impact and validate the information shared.

The next step is to bring both parties together for a facilitated discussion, where the founder should establish ground rules up front. Rich has seen conflict escalate when the structure for their discussion is not clarified. This can lead to defensiveness, miscommunication, and unproductive arguments. Examples of ground rules: no interruptions, focus on solutions and not blame, everyone gets equal time to speak. Rather than shying away from the role of facilitator, founders should realize the power they have and the tone that they set. By learning how to mediate conversation and reframe emotionally charged statements into constructive ones, the founder can guide the team toward shared goals and actionable resolutions.

Always be following up.

Again and again throughout this book, we've stressed the value of cadence (we try to practice what we preach). Even if you think you've figured something out, problems tend to metastasize in a vacuum. Without follow-up, resolutions may lose their effectiveness, allowing old issues to resurface. By scheduling periodic check-ins, you can gauge the effectiveness of the resolution, address lingering concerns, and offer additional support as needed. Cadence also helps resolve issues *before* they escalate. Establish clear channels for feedback and grievances. Don't phone in your regular team meetings. They're a great opportunity to promote open, honest conversation.

■　■　■

Ultimately, a founder's ability to handle conflicts constructively not only resolves immediate tensions but also models a culture of collaboration and accountability within the team. If you handle conflicts effectively, you will garner the emotional and intellectual buy-in that supports a cohesive work environment where challenges are addressed openly and solutions are created collectively. As always, you need to be good at many things—developing empathy, establishing clear processes, following up rigorously. But if you face this admittedly uncomfortable task head-on, you will not just be able to prevent minor issues from escalating but also support a resilient, innovative organization that's ready to tackle the complexities of growth and competition.

CHAPTER 16

The Path to a Billion: Developing Structure, Systems, and Processes

If you're in charge of one of the 13% of startups that manage to reach $10 million in ARR after 10 years of existence, congratulations. You've reached the traction stage. You've hired great people. You've created a culture of smart, expeditious decision-making. You've learned how to master the triangle of execution: delegation, accountability, and coaching. Your executive group operates like a real team, with each person bringing their unique perspective to create a jointly owned strategy that is aligned with your vision.

Hopefully, some of the concepts in this book have helped with that tremendous effort. But now you have your eye on the prize: an IPO, followed by a billion-dollar run rate.

But there's one last challenge to face. It's particularly dangerous, because it's invisible, like the nitrogen in the air we breathe. It's not a screamingly apparent obstacle, so much as a deeply pernicious *absence*. If you're not careful, it can kill you in your sleep. It's the hidden time bomb that blows up founder after founder: inattention (or outright aversion) to structure, systems, and processes.

Let's take a second to define these three core competencies:

- **Structure:** Think of this as your company's org chart: who does what, who reports to whom, what is the composition of each team, and how decisions get made. Without it, no one knows who's in charge of what, and things get messy fast.
- **Systems:** These are the tools and tech that make everything run smoothly. It could be your Slack channels, project management software like Asana, or even your CRM. Systems make sure stuff gets done the same way every time without you micromanaging.
- **Processes:** These are the step-by-step instructions for how things get done. Like a playbook for hiring, onboarding, product launches—whatever. Having processes in place means you don't have to reinvent the wheel every time something comes up.

That's all fine and well. But here's the problem: Founders are psychically engineered to attack the status quo. As a result, they have a deeply ingrained suspicion of anything that smacks of an excessively complicated administrative process. They see systems as bureaucracy. What is bureaucracy? Rich has a very simple definition: Layers of policies and procedures that no longer have any meaning and slow everybody down. The word derives from *bureau*, or a chest of drawers (presumably stuffed with soul-crushing documents in triplicate). It's a founder's worst nightmare.

But when a company is at scale, a founder's aversion to structure, systems, and processes can lead to chaos. People don't know what they're doing, resources get wasted, and your growth hits a wall. Just look at the 360 comments: "He tends to brute-force projects by default rather than identifying scalable processes and systems," "Never really set up a process, or if we do, it gets changed constantly," "He makes it clear he has zero patience for structure, systems, or processes," etc.

You get the general idea. Their long-suffering board members tend to break down this general antipathy toward process into the following components:

- Lack of consistency and follow-through
- Overreliance on others and delegation
- Resistance to structure and preference for flexibility
- Inadequate understanding of organizational needs
- Failure to communicate and collaborate on process development
- Inability to balance short-term and long-term needs

Think about the conversations you've had with board members and key advisors over the years. Have any of the above bullets come up as repeated themes? If so, you may have a problem with systems and processes. Taken together, these issues describe a founder who has hit traction stage but has yet to conquer these last critical competencies. As a result, they are desperately trying to swim upstream against a raging current of complexity.

To help founders get in touch with the issue, Rich has a standard set of questions that he asks his founders: Do you see the same problems happening over and over again? Do you have certain kinds of fire drills that happen on a repeat basis? Are there particular mistakes that just refuse to go away? Do brute-force, manual processes take up a lot of time? Do you see new employees struggling to get up to speed because they lack the necessary playbooks or documentation? They tend to sigh and answer glumly in the affirmative. The fiery "tear it all down" attitude fades fast.

Here's a hard truth about startups: The further you progress, the harder it gets. The race actually *speeds up*. Once you get into traction stage, the complexity of the system is going to outstrip your ability to effectively respond to individual crises: new markets, new dependencies, new customer and stakeholder demands. If you want to build a sustainable business, you're going to have to figure out how to effectively manage more volume and more complexity. Hoping for all the problems to simply "go away" is not a sound business strategy.

Founders frequently confuse crisis-driven processes with growth-oriented processes. What's the difference? In the early days of a startup, you're often lurching from crisis to crisis. What is your reward for deftly handling each emergency? Survival. So quick, ad hoc processes like agile scrums or emergency client calls constitute your basic modus operandi. Growth-oriented processes, on the other hand, are about anticipating complexity, streamlining operations, and building the automation platforms you need in order to generate steady revenue. They are the operational spine your company needs to help it scale and soar. These processes are about efficiency, yes, but they're also about *opportunity*.

10 Questions: How to Develop Systems and Processes

1. Do you have the necessary systems in place to support your company's growth, or are you constantly scrambling to put out fires?
2. Do you proactively plan to grow and develop your in-house systems, or do you wait for issues to arise before taking action?
3. Are your company's processes aligned with its strategic goals, or have they become disconnected over time? How would you even know?
4. Do you regularly gather feedback on your systems to identify bottlenecks, or do you assume they're working as intended?
5. Are you clear on the key metrics and KPIs that guide your company's performance, or is success measured informally?
6. How intentional are you about balancing structure with flexibility, allowing for innovation without sacrificing order?
7. Do you document your standard operating procedures and make them accessible to your team, or is knowledge primarily shared informally?
8. How rigorously do you assess whether each system and process adds value? Do unused or outdated tools clutter your operations?
9. Do you invest in training and support for your team on new systems, or do you expect them to adapt on their own?
10. Are you creating a scalable organizational structure that clearly defines roles and responsibilities, or does your team operate with ambiguous boundaries?

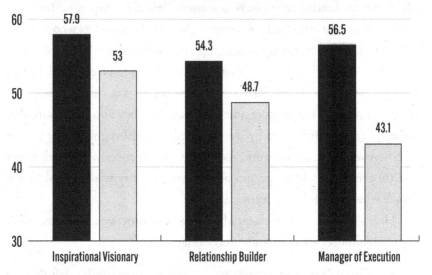

Execution Through Systems: The Ultimate Differentiator

How important are structure, systems, and processes to your overall success as a founder?

Let's return to the Three Pillars of Leadership. We know that most founders tend to index higher on inspirational vision. But how important, you may ask, is execution? Well, as it turns out, it's much more important than you might think.

The chart above appears to compare two sets of founders—successful on the left, and unsuccessful on the right. But it doesn't—it's indexed on execution. It compares a group of founders who rank above average on Manager of Execution skills (56.5) versus those who rank below average (43.1). But, as you can see, a high rank on ME correlates to *a high rank on everything else*. For most successful founders, execution is the anchor pillar, the key differentiator between success and failure.

Not surprisingly, the founders that index higher on execution also rank higher on structure, systems, and processes. These leaders simply get better results. They are much better at implementing and executing the systems and processes needed to generate consistent, relatable outcomes. By minimizing chaos and optimizing resources, they are the founders who successfully transition from startup to scale-up. They defuse the time bomb.

These founders understand that you put systems in place in order to *get ahead of complexity*. If you sharpen the saw before you cut the wood, the work will proceed much more quickly. Crucially, they also make sure that these systems are informed by the frustrations and insights of the people who have to do the actual work. As a result, these processes (a) work better and (b) generate more usage and buy-in, because they were shaped by the people who use them on a regular basis.

Here are some of the essential systems and processes that execution-oriented founders are constantly developing:

- **Organizational structure:** As the team expands, defining an organizational structure becomes imperative. This involves delineating clear roles and responsibilities, establishing reporting lines, and creating departments or teams focused on specific functions such as marketing, sales, product development, and customer support. A well-defined organizational structure helps in avoiding confusion, preventing overlaps, and ensuring accountability.

- **Standard operating procedures (SOPs):** Documenting SOPs for critical operations ensures consistency and efficiency. SOPs provide step-by-step instructions for routine tasks, helping new employees get up to speed quickly and reducing the risk of errors. For instance, having SOPs for customer onboarding, sales processes, and product development cycles can streamline operations and enhance productivity. That doesn't mean you have to create those SOPs on your own—you just need to signal their importance to the rest of the company and elevate the folks who do this well.

- **Financial management systems:** Implementing robust financial management systems is essential as financial transactions become more complex. This includes budgeting, forecasting, and financial reporting tools that provide real-time insights into the company's financial health. Effective financial management helps in making informed decisions, securing additional funding, and ensuring regulatory compliance.

- **Project management tools:** Utilizing project management tools like Trello, Asana, or Jira helps in organizing tasks, tracking progress, and managing deadlines. These tools facilitate collaboration, enhance visibility into the status of projects, and ensure that teams are working efficiently toward common goals.

- **Performance metrics and KPIs:** Establishing key performance indicators (KPIs) and metrics to monitor progress is crucial for scaling. KPIs provide measurable benchmarks that help in evaluating the effectiveness of strategies and making data-driven decisions. Metrics related to customer acquisition cost (CAC), lifetime value (LTV), churn rate, and revenue growth are particularly important.

- **Human resources systems:** As the team grows, having structured HR processes for recruitment, onboarding, performance evaluation, and employee development becomes vital. HR systems help in attracting top talent, retaining employees, and fostering a positive organizational culture.

Proactively developing these systems and processes is not just about maintaining order; it's about creating a foundation for sustainable growth. Airbnb's early implementation of a robust customer support system, for example, allowed it to handle a rapidly increasing user base without compromising service quality. Slack's use of performance metrics and iterative development processes enabled it to scale effectively while continuously improving its product. Without these systems in place, these companies would have drowned in their own growth.

To summarize: Why are structure, systems, and processes so crucial to scaling effectively?

- **Clarity and accountability:** Everyone knows what's expected of them. There's less confusion, fewer dropped balls.
- **Consistency and quality control:** You can repeat what works without constantly being involved. That's how you keep your customers happy.
- **Sane scalability:** Growth doesn't have to inevitably lead to burnout. Processes and systems make that growth much more manageable.
- **Quicker decisions:** With systems in place, your managers can make decisions without waiting for you to sign off on everything.
- **Culture preservation:** As you grow, processes help preserve what makes your company unique.

Advice: How to Develop Systems and Processes

Be proactive. Anticipate.

Don't wait for problems to arise before addressing process issues. Be proactive in identifying and solving potential issues. That being said, you need to avoid getting involved in every detail of process implementation and trust your team to handle operational tasks. Hire operational leaders who complement your visionary strength. Delegate responsibility for specific processes to them, and empower them to make decisions within their domain. Move away from making decisions based solely on gut feelings; instead, use data and analysis to inform your decisions. Ask yourself: Based on the data available, where do I want to be six months from now? A year from now? Three years from now? Do I have the systems and processes in place to support those goals?

Pursue better living through feedback.

> It begins with an idea, which is translated into a product via the "build stage." When customers interact with that product, they create data, which startups harvest in the "measure stage." And, with any luck, that data will inform the company in the "learn stage," and that learning will influence the next set of ideas. This three-stage

*feedback loop sounds simple, but it's powerful nonetheless. It gives
rise to this heuristic for evaluating any process or infrastructure
change in the context of a startup:* Always choose the option
that minimizes the total time through the feedback loop.
—Eric Reiss[1]

The same feedback processes for building your product apply to managing your systems. All systems benefit from feedback and usage data. The best ones become *more* relevant and useful with every turn of the feedback wheel. Gathering data-driven insights can help you identify bottlenecks and areas for improvement. Regular reviews help maintain the relevance and effectiveness of processes as the organization evolves. Create channels for feedback from employees at all levels and encourage collaborative efforts to improve processes.

Align everything.

Processes should not exist for their own sake. Most companies now have dozens of SaaS (software as a service) solutions, all clamoring for more usage (that's how their vendors make money). But your company isn't going to succeed or fail based on how much you use a given system. You need to make sure that everything is working toward your overall strategic goals. If you're launching a new system, be transparent and explain your reasons so that the team gets buy-in. Stay aware of the cost of the "care and feeding" of your SaaS systems. Watch out for unnecessary complexity. Avoid making process changes in isolation without considering their impact on other areas of the organization.

Feed it or kill it.

A startup needs to balance flexibility with discipline. If a given system is not being used much, or if it's not furthering your strategic goals, *get rid of it.* Schedule regular reviews of your systems and processes to identify areas for improvement and ensure they remain aligned with organizational goals. Make sure that everything is well documented and easily accessible—it's the only way to make sure a given system is used effectively. Don't dismiss feedback from your team about existing processes. Take their input seriously and make necessary adjustments.

Don't overlook the human element.
Feature overload applies to humans as well as applications. Do not overlook the impact of processes on your team. Heavy-handed implementations can hurt morale and hit productivity. The idea is to leverage technology in order to make things *easier for everyone* by reducing manual effort and streamlining tasks. Don't underestimate the importance of training or assume that team members inherently know how to follow or improve processes. Provide adequate training and support. Continuous training ensures that everyone is on the same page and capable of executing processes effectively.

■ ■ ■

As you move forward, remember that *every system you implement is a step toward transforming your vision into reality.* Build wisely, iterate relentlessly, and never lose sight of the balance between order and creativity. You're the visionary—your company's creative engine. But for that vision to grow, you need structure to support it. You need scaffolding. This isn't about stifling creativity; it's about amplifying your impact. Bring in the right people, build discipline, and set up the processes that make your company run like a well-oiled machine. This is how you scale without losing your spark. This is how you fly.

APPENDIX

Hagberg's 46 Competencies

Hagberg's 46 Competencies derive from the 360 assessments of leadership capabilities of almost 2,000 executives from multiple industries and in multiple countries. Most of the people rated are senior executives and were rated by an average of 12 raters each. Raters included their direct manager, their direct reports, board members, advisors, and other employees. Each rater was presented with a precisely worded definition of each of the 46 competencies and rated the executive on a 1–5 scale. Each rater was asked to gauge the relative importance of each competency to the executive's performance in their job. Raters were also given the opportunity to make written comments on each of the 46 competencies.

The typical executive received an average of 35 pages of comments and a quantitative report that presented an analysis of the numerical ratings in multiple ways. The "Importance Ratings" were also compared to the "Performance Ratings," yielding a "Gap Analysis" between things that were important and the person's actual rating. These were used to identify potential developmental issues that could guide goal setting.

If these 46 competencies are derived from business executives in general, then why should they apply to founders more specifically? For a very simple reason: *All of Rich's founder clients express a desire to scale with their company.* These are the competencies that are required to grow a large organization, as exhibited by leaders who have successfully accomplished that monumental task.

The 46 competencies are as following:

Adaptability—Adapts to rapidly changing situations and priorities, tolerates ambiguity, and develops new ways of behaving in order to achieve objectives and get around obstacles.

Agent of Change—Challenges the status quo, supports fresh perspectives, tries out new approaches, and enlists support for change initiatives.

Assertiveness—Makes requests and expresses beliefs, feelings, and needs in a direct, honest, and appropriate way that respects the rights of others.

Building Partnerships—Works effectively with other groups and functions, shares information across the enterprise, and considers the impact of decisions on other departments and groups.

Building Teams—Models and encourages teamwork by fostering cooperation, communication, trust, shared goals, interdependency, and mutual accountability and support.

Coaching—Facilitates career development of subordinates by providing regular coaching. Helps them change behavior, improve performance, and sustain commitment through encouragement, support, collaborative problem-solving, goal setting, and feedback.

Creating Buy-In—Effectively builds commitment and wins support for initiatives through personal and professional credibility, trustworthiness, persuasive communication, stakeholder involvement, and by aligning expectations.

Creating Meaning—Ties day-to-day actions of individuals to a higher meaning and to the broad strategic priorities of the organization, giving a more expansive significance to work activities.

Creativity and Innovation—Personally generates new or improved ideas, approaches, products, or solutions.

Culture Management—Displays a genuine passion for nurturing a culture and proactively aligning the organization's culture to support its vision strategy and core values.

Decisiveness—Makes clear-cut decisions without unnecessary delay, even in tough situations.

Delegation and Empowerment—Places trust in others by moving decision-making close to the level where the work is done and by giving others the responsibility, authority, independence, and support they need to succeed.

Dependability—Can be counted on to meet commitments and deadlines.

Developing Structures, Systems, and Processes—Designs and establishes structures, systems, and processes to most effectively achieve the organization's objectives.

Emotional Control and Composure—Maintains composure during times of stress, pressure, or disagreement; avoids unproductive confrontation and maintains a positive outlook in the face of adversity.

Emphasizing Excellence—Sets challenging goals and high standards of excellence, while refusing to accept mediocre or substandard performance.

External Focus—Keeps up on developments outside the organization that may have an impact on the business, such as trends in the industry, new technologies, and events in the larger economic and political environments.

Facilitating Conflict Resolution—Facilitates conflict resolution between coworkers by surfacing and clarifying areas of disagreement and by creating an environment where resolution is possible.

Finding and Attracting Talent—Commits time and energy to the hiring process and makes good hiring decisions. Identifies talented, high-quality job candidates and successfully brings them into the organization.

First Impression—Creates a positive first impression through social confidence, dress, sincerity, and a professional self-presentation.

Formal Presentation—Delivers poised, interesting, high-impact, informative, and organized presentations that meet the expectations and needs of the audience.

Forthrightness—Is sincere, genuine, open, and direct with others. Has no hidden agenda.

Handling Resistance to Change—Identifies sources of resistance to change and effectively deals with them before they undermine change initiatives.

Holding People Accountable—Clarifies expectations and holds people accountable for getting results; objectively measures outcomes against established goals while rewarding achievement and confronting poor performance.

Information Sharing—Openly shares information with colleagues, keeping them in the loop about plans, activities, objectives, recent developments, and progress toward goals.

Inspirational Role Model—Gives others within the organization hope and inspiration by displaying optimism, energy, confidence, enthusiasm, determination, and commitment, especially in tough times.

Judgment and Reasoning—Effectively diagnoses problems, identifies core issues, exercises common sense, sees critical connections and ramifications, and analyzes alternatives.

Leveraging Diversity—Actively builds and manages a workforce that is diverse in ideas, backgrounds, culture, ethnicity, gender, and disciplines.

Listening—Listens attentively, doesn't interrupt, accurately hears what is said, asks questions to clarify meaning, communicates understanding, and shows interest.

Model of Commitment—Consistently sets a standard of dedication, hard work, energy, and commitment.

Model of Values—Engenders respect from others through consistent moral and ethical behavior, high standards of personal conduct, and promoting and modeling the principles and values that are central to the success of the organization.

Negotiation—Negotiates win-win outcomes by being well prepared, gaining trust, searching for creative and mutually beneficial solutions, and being willing to compromise when appropriate.

Openness to Input—Solicits and is open to feedback and differing ideas and views; avoids intimidation or domination; and welcomes suggestions.

Organizational Awareness—Is alert to events and trends within the organization and considers how they might influence the long-term performance of the organization.

Planning, Prioritizing, and Maintaining Focus—Establishes short-term goals, clarifies roles and responsibilities, sets priorities and milestones, and is not distracted by unimportant details or activities.

Praise and Recognition—Recognizes, praises, and rewards others for good performance.

Re-engineering Processes—Identifies inefficiencies and recurring problems, and restructures the organization to maximize effectiveness.

Relationship Building—Is friendly, open, and approachable; cultivates trusting relationships that are maintained over time.

Resilience and Stress Management—Copes well with the stress and the demands of the job, maintaining energy, strength, and endurance; rebounds quickly from setbacks and perseveres in the face of adversity.

Results and Productivity—Gets results, accomplishes objectives, and sees projects to completion.

Self-Confidence—Demonstrates strong, realistic confidence in themself and their powers and abilities.

Sensitivity and Consideration—Shows respect for others and is sensitive to their needs, concerns, and perspectives.

Social Astuteness—Accurately reads and responds astutely and diplomatically in dealing with others; understands the social dynamics of the work group and the larger organization.

Strategic Focus—Thinks strategically; creates an ongoing, dynamic, strategic planning process; and communicates the organization's long-term direction.

Taking Initiative—Takes the initiative to identify problems and opportunities, and assumes a leadership role by taking action without being asked.

Visionary Thinking—Creates and communicates a clear, coherent, and compelling image of what the organization strives to become; enthusiastically presents a target for the future that is energizing and inspiring; and provides a sense of future direction.

ACKNOWLEDGMENTS

I would like to thank the incredible employees who were part of the companies I've founded. In researching and writing this book, I came to see just how closely the founder's journey mirrored my own personality and choices—fitting me like a well-worn glove. If only hindsight could rewrite history; I would certainly have done some things differently with the wisdom I hold now.

To Melissa Guzy of Arbor Ventures: Thank you for your unwavering support and for opening my eyes to how a founder's personality and leadership style profoundly influence financial outcomes. Your expertise and guidance have been indispensable in connecting the dots between data and human behavior.

This book would not have been possible without the efforts of Senthil Ramaswamy and Shay Gipson.

Finally, to my wife, Tori: Your patience and grace as I disappeared into the depths of writing have been nothing short of heroic. Thank you for standing by me during the years when this book consumed so much of my attention. Your love and understanding have been my anchor.

—Rich

We might be lone wolves by nature, but the founder's journey is never a solitary one. I am incredibly fortunate to have been surrounded by people who encouraged and supported me in my early founder's journey. To Marc Benioff, Mike Braun, and Peter Fenton: Thank you for encouraging me to take the plunge. To my early board members, including Jason Pressman, Scott Thompson, Tim Haley, and Mike Volpi: You helped keep me on track when the road was not clear. Thanks to Steve Humphreys, Rene Cirulli, Mary Hartman, Tyler Sloat, and Richard Terry-Lloyd for bringing out my best self. To Gabe, who brings my thoughts to life on the printed page, and to Dana for the hard work of midwifing three headstrong authors through a very personal journey. And finally, to all the ZEOs who believed in our vision and mission.

—Tien

NOTES

Introduction

1. "Press Release: Former Start-Up CEO Charged in $175 Million Fraud," US Attorney's Office, Southern District of New York, April 4, 2023, https://www .justice.gov/usao-sdny/pr/former-start-ceo-charged-175-million-fraud.
2. Pete Syme, "Forbes Built a Hall of Shame for All the Questionable People on Its 30 Under 30 Lists," *Business Insider*, November 29, 2023, https://www.business insider.com/forbes-hall-shame-30-under-30-lists-regrets-sbf-ftx-2023-11.
3. Anthony DeMarco, "Baume & Mercier Presents Forbes 'Doers Award' to Elizabeth Holmes," *Forbes*, October 6, 2015, https://www.forbes.com/sites /anthonydemarco/2015/10/05/baume-mercier-presents-forbes-doers-award-to -elizabeth-holmes/.
4. "Press Release: Trevor Milton Sentenced to Four Years in Prison for Securities Fraud Scheme," US Attorney's Office, Southern District of New York, December 18, 2023, https://www.justice.gov/usao-sdny/pr/trevor-milton-sentenced-four -years-prison-securities-fraud-scheme.
5. Gideon Lewis-Kraus, "Will Sam Bankman-Fried's Guilty Verdict Change Anything?," *New Yorker*, November 3, 2023, https://www.newyorker.com/news /our-local-correspondents/the-trials-of-sam-bankman-fried.
6. Elizabeth Pollman, "Startup Failure," Harvard Law School Forum on Corporate Governance, September 29, 2023, https://corpgov.law.harvard.edu/2023/09/29 /startup-failure/.
7. Noam Wasserman, "The Founder's Dilemma," *Harvard Business Review*, February 1, 2008, https://hbr.org/2008/02/the-founders-dilemma.

8. Peter Vanham and Nicholas Gordon, "Fortune's New Global 500 List Shows Europe's Decline, the U.S.'s Rise," *Fortune*, August 3, 2023, https://fortune.com/2023/08/03/fortunes-new-global-500-list-europe-decline-us-rise/.

Chapter 1

1. "Steve Jobs Fired Me 5 Times and I Still Loved Working with Him," YouTube video, posted by Insider Tech, December 2, 2017, https://www.youtube.com/watch?v=2DmHWIwPjKA.
2. Neil Theise, *Notes on Complexity: A Scientific Theory of Connection, Consciousness, and Being* (New York: Spiegel & Grau, 2023).
3. Jeff Bezos, "2016 Letter to Shareholders," *About Amazon* (blog), April 17, 2017, https://www.aboutamazon.com/news/company-news/2016-letter-to-shareholders.
4. Kurt Vonnegut, *Player Piano* (New York: Dial Press, 2009).

Chapter 2

1. Ali Tamaseb, *Super Founders: What Data Reveals About Billion-Dollar Startups* (New York: PublicAffairs, 2021); Pierre Azoulay, Benjamin F. Jones, J. Daniel Kim, and Javier Miranda, "Research: The Average Age of a Successful Startup Founder Is 45," *Harvard Business Review*, July 11, 2018, https://hbr.org/2018/07/research-the-average-age-of-a-successful-startup-founder-is-45.
2. Frederic Kerrest, *Zero to IPO: Over $1 Trillion of Actionable Advice from the World's Most Successful Entrepreneurs* (New York: McGraw-Hill, 2022).

Chapter 3

1. Eliot Brown and Maureen Farrell, *The Cult of We: WeWork, Adam Neumann, and the Great Startup Delusion* (New York: Crown, 2021).
2. Erin Griffith, "The End of Faking It in Silicon Valley," *New York Times*, April 15, 2023, https://www.nytimes.com/2023/04/15/business/silicon-valley-fraud.html.
3. Mike Wilson, *The Difference Between God and Larry Ellison: Inside Oracle Corporation* (New York: Harper Business, 2003).
4. Jim Shleckser, "Why Netflix Doesn't Tolerate Brilliant Jerks," *Inc.*, February 2, 2016, https://www.inc.com/jim-schleckser/why-netflix-doesn-t-tolerate-brilliant-jerks.html.
5. Marc Andreessen, "Investing in Flow," *a16z.com* (blog), August 15, 2022, https://a16z.com/announcement/investing-in-flow/.

Chapter 4

1. Stephen Covey, *The 7 Habits of Highly Effective People* (New York: Simon & Schuster, 2020).
2. Matt Blumberg, *Startup CEO: A Field Guide to Scaling Up Your Business* (New York: Wiley, 2020).
3. Shunryu Suzuki, *Zen Mind, Beginner's Mind* (Boulder: Shambhala Publications, 2006).

Chapter 5

1. Malcolm Gladwell, *David and Goliath: Underdogs, Misfits, and the Art of Battling Giants* (New York: Little, Brown, 2013).
2. Patrick Lencioni, *The Five Dysfunctions of a Team: A Leadership Fable* (New York: Jossey-Bass, 2002); Simon Sinek, *Leaders Eat Last: Why Some Teams Pull Together and Others Don't* (New York: Portfolio, 2014); Daniel Coyle, *The Culture Code: The Secrets of Highly Successful Groups* (New York: Bantam, 2018).
3. Paul Graham, "Founder Mode," September 2024, accessed December 13, 2024, https://paulgraham.com/foundermode.html.
4. Jason Calacanis, host, *This Week in Startups*, podcast, episode 1735, "Airbnb CEO Brian Chesky on early rejection, customer focus & AI's future in hospitality," May 4, 2023, https://creators.spotify.com/pod/show/thisweekinstartups/episodes/Airbnb-CEO-Brian-Chesky-on-early-rejection--customer-focus--AIs-future-in-hospitality--E1735-e23gc1i.
5. Reid Hoffman and Ben Casnocha, *The Startup of You: Adapt, Take Risks, Grow Your Network, and Transform Your Career* (New York: Crown Currency, 2012).
6. Yuval Noah Harari, *Sapiens: A Brief History of Humankind* (New York: Harper, 2015).
7. Daniel Goleman, *Emotional Intelligence: Why It Can Matter More Than IQ* (New York: Bantam, 2012).

Chapter 6

1. Eric Ries, "For Startups, How Much Process Is Too Much?" *Harvard Business Review*, February 24, 2010, https://hbr.org/2010/02/how-much-process-is-too-much.
2. Michael E. Gerber, *The E-Myth Revisited: Why Most Small Businesses Don't Work and What to Do About It* (New York: HarperCollins, 2009).

3. Ranjay Gulati and Alicia DeSantola, "Start-Ups That Last," *Harvard Business Review*, March 2016, https://hbr.org/2016/03/start-ups-that-last.

Chapter 7

1. Robert Sapolsky, "The Psychology of Stress," YouTube video, posted by Greater Good Science Center, March 20, 2012, https://www.youtube.com/watch?v=bEcdGK4DQSg.
2. Peter Drucker, "The Effective Decision," *Harvard Business Review*, January 1967, https://hbr.org/1967/01/the-effective-decision.
3. Sam Altman, "Founder Depression," *SamAltman.com* (blog), June 13, 2014, https://blog.samaltman.com/founder-depression.
4. Simon Baron-Cohen, *Zero Degrees of Empathy: A New Understanding of Cruelty and Kindness* (New York: Penguin, 2012).
5. Ben Horowitz, *The Hard Thing About Hard Things: Building a Business When There Are No Easy Answers* (New York: Harper Business, 2014).
6. Bret Waters, "Startup Founder Integrity," *Medium* (blog), September 8, 2021, https://medium.com/the-launch-path/startup-founder-integrity-58d50ddbdd9d.
7. Mike Isaac, *Super Pumped: The Battle for Uber* (New York: W. W. Norton, 2019).

Chapter 8

1. Anthony K. Tjan, "How Leaders Become Self-Aware," *Harvard Business Review*, July 19, 2012, https://hbr.org/2012/07/how-leaders-become-self-aware.
2. Carter Cast and Brooke Vuckovic, "How Founders Self-Destruct Under Pressure," *Harvard Business Review*, September 9, 2022, https://hbr.org/2022/09/how-founders-self-destruct-under-pressure.
3. Mark Kermode, "David Lynch," *The Guardian*, February 8, 2007, https://www.theguardian.com/film/2007/feb/08/davidlynch.

Chapter 9

1. Daniel Kahneman, *Thinking, Fast and Slow* (New York: Farrar, Straus and Giroux, 2011).
2. Kahneman, *Thinking, Fast and Slow*.
3. Kahneman, *Thinking, Fast and Slow*.
4. Kahneman, *Thinking, Fast and Slow*.

5. Sir Andrew Likierman, "The Elements of Good Judgment," *Harvard Business Review*, January–February 2020, https://hbr.org/2020/01/the-elements-of-good -judgment.

6. Jon Victor, "Databricks' 'Truth-Seeking' CEO Wants to Be Bigger Than Sales-force," The Information, December 2, 2024, https://www.theinformation.com /articles/databricks-truth-seeking-ceo-wants-to-be-bigger-than-salesforce.

7. Yogi Berra, *The Yogi Book* (New York: Workman, 1999).

8. "Warren on staying rational and avoiding confirmation bias," YouTube video, posted by Euprime, November 11, 2021, https://www.youtube.com/watch?v =NLKNsU3tI0E.

9. Reid Hoffman, June Cohen, and Deron Triff, *Masters of Scale: Surprising Truths from the World's Most Successful Entrepreneurs* (New York: Crown Currency, 2021).

Chapter 10

1. Eric Van den Steen, "Strategy and Strategic Decisions," Harvard Business School Technical Note, 712-500, June 2012 (Revised December 2017), https:// www.hbs.edu/faculty/Pages/item.aspx?num=42596.

2. Peter Drucker, *The Effective Executive: The Definitive Guide to Getting the Right Things Done* (New York: Harper Business, 2017).

3. "Management by Walking Around," Hewlett-Packard Company Archives Virtual Vault, https://www.hewlettpackardhistory.com/item/management-by-walking -around/.

4. Rick Klau, "How Google Sets Goals: OKRs," *Google Ventures Library* (blog), October 25, 2012, https://library.gv.com/how-google-sets-goals-okrs-a1f69b0b72c7.

5. John Doerr, *Measure What Matters: How Google, Bono, and the Gates Foundation Rock the World with OKRs* (New York: Portfolio, 2018).

6. Project Management Institute, *Agile Practice Guide* (Newtown Square: Project Management Institute, 2017).

Chapter 11

1. Stephen Covey, *The 7 Habits of Highly Effective People* (New York: Simon & Schuster, 2020).

2. Eliyahu M. Goldratt and Jeff Cox, *The Goal: A Process of Ongoing Improvement* (Great Barrington: North River Press, 2004).

3. Jim Schleckser, *Great CEOs Are Lazy* (New York: Inc. Original Imprint, 2016).

Chapter 12

1. D. Watkins, "5 Life-Changing Lessons from Larry David," Salon, March 24, 2024, https://www.salon.com/2024/03/24/curb-your-enthusiasm-lessons-larry -david/.

Chapter 13

1. "Steve Jobs on *60 Minutes*," YouTube video, posted by Mac History, March 31, 2012, https://www.youtube.com/watch?v=pGvnJJxBAlc.
2. Ken Blanchard and Randy Conley, *Simple Truths of Leadership: 52 Ways to Be a Servant Leader and Build Trust* (Oakland: Berrett-Koehler, 2022).
3. Alex Pentland, "The New Science of Building Great Teams," *Harvard Business Review*, April 2012, https://hbr.org/2012/04/the-new-science-of-building-great -teams.
4. Paul Rogers and Marcia W. Blenko, "Who Has the D?: How Clear Decision Roles Enhance Organizational Performance," *Harvard Business Review*, January 2006, https://hbr.org/2006/01/who-has-the-d-how-clear-decision-roles-enhance -organizational-performance.

Chapter 14

1. Tim Bajarin, "How Steve Jobs Helped Guarantee Tim Cook's Success at Apple," *Forbes*, September 2, 2021, https://www.forbes.com/sites/timbajarin/2021/09/02 /how-steve-jobs-helped-guarantee-tim-cooks-success-at-apple/.
2. Bajarin, "How Steve Jobs Helped Guarantee Tim Cook's Success."
3. Bajarin, "How Steve Jobs Helped Guarantee Tim Cook's Success."
4. Patty McCord, "How Netflix Reinvented HR," *Harvard Business Review*, January 2014, https://hbr.org/2014/01/how-netflix-reinvented-hr.
5. Brian Chesky, 2024 interview with Lenny Rachitsky, LinkedIn post, accessed December 13, 2024, https://www.linkedin.com/posts/lennyrachitsky_brian -cheskyon-how-being-in-the-details-activity-7238256618734264320-4iV8.

Chapter 16

1. Eric Reiss, *Usable Usability: Simple Steps for Making Stuff Better* (New York: Wiley, 2012).

INDEX

ABOUT THE AUTHORS

Dr. Rich Hagberg is a consulting psychologist and leadership expert with over 45 years of experience advising more than 500 companies worldwide. With a career rooted in Silicon Valley, Rich holds a BA from UCLA and a PhD in counseling psychology from Washington State University. Rich spent three decades working with some of the most prominent tech firms before shifting his focus in 2009 to coaching startup founders and their teams. An entrepreneur himself, Rich has founded multiple companies, including HCG, Inc., which he led for 22 years before its acquisition by Accenture.

Tien Tzuo is a successful founder, a best-selling author, and a software startup junkie. The creator of the phrase "the subscription economy," Tien cofounded Zuora in 2008 to help companies launch and manage recurring revenue–based business models and successfully took the company public on the New York Stock Exchange in 2018. He is the author of the national bestseller *Subscribed: Why the Subscription Model Will Be Your Company's Future—and What to Do About It*. Prior to founding Zuora, Tien joined Salesforce as its 11th hire and rose to Chief Marketing Officer and then Chief Strategy Officer. Tien holds a BS from Cornell and an MBA from Stanford and is a prolific angel investor and founder mentor.